T0099939

He♡rtgasm!

Increasing Intimacy & Ecstasy with Your Beloved

by Best-Selling Author,
Toni De Marco

Front Cover Photo by
Juan le Parc

BALBOA
PRESS
A DIVISION OF HAY HOUSE

Copyright © 2013 Toni De Marco

All rights reserved. No part of this book may be used or reproduced by
any means, graphic, electronic, or mechanical, including photocopying,
recording, taping or by any information storage retrieval system
without the written permission of the publisher except in the case
of brief quotations embodied in critical articles and reviews.

ISBN: 978-1-4525-5603-1 (sc)
ISBN: 978-1-4525-5602-4 (hc)
ISBN: 978-1-4525-5611-6 (e)

Library of Congress Control Number: 2012913263

Balboa Press books may be ordered through booksellers or by contacting:
Balboa Press
A Division of Hay House
1663 Liberty Drive
Bloomington, IN 47403
www.balboapress.com
1-(877) 407-4847

Because of the dynamic nature of the Internet, any web addresses or
links contained in this book may have changed since publication and
may no longer be valid. The views expressed in this work are solely those
of the author and do not necessarily reflect the views of the publisher,
and the publisher hereby disclaims any responsibility for them.

The author of this book does not dispense medical advice or prescribe
the use of any technique as a form of treatment for physical, emotional,
or medical problems without the advice of a physician, either directly
or indirectly. The intent of the author is only to offer information
of a general nature to help you in your quest for emotional and
spiritual well-being. In the event you use any of the information in
this book for yourself, which is your constitutional right, the author
and the publisher assume no responsibility for your actions.

Any people depicted in stock imagery provided by Thinkstock are
models, and such images are being used for illustrative purposes only.
Certain stock imagery © Thinkstock.

Printed in the United States of America

Balboa Press rev. date: 02/15/2013

Contents

Scene 1: Healing with Communication & Creating Intimacy by Enhancing Your Heart Connection

Scene 4: Ramping Up Your Juiciness by Feeling the Difference Between Male & Female Energy

Scene 5: Trusting Your Passion as You Learn
Orgasmic Response and Build Your Ecstatic Energy

Author Prefix

This book evolved out of the intensive 3-day trainings that I've traveled all over the world facilitating for people who, a lot like myself, were lost in relationship hell. "HE♥RTGASM!" guides you through an abbreviated process in which you can build an understanding of how to get to relationship heaven. In this virtual workshop/book, you will experience a reality-based awakening process, which helps to explain the concepts you are being presented.

There have been many teachers and workshop facilitators who have contributed to my own training and journey, many in very significant ways, and when appropriate, I will mention their names and contributions throughout this book.

Through my travels, an idea emerged as a way to suggest the sequence that successful relationships follow: First you learn to relate to yourself, then you learn to love your partner, and then you are positioned to have an amazing sex life.

It took me four years to finish this book. And, it was almost a year after that, when attending a Robert Allen seminar on creating your book title, that I came up with "HE♥RTGASM!" as the title for my book. It was just "downloaded," right into my mind, immediately followed by the subtitle, "Increasing Intimacy & Ecstasy with Your Beloved." People clapped and cheered when they heard the title so I decided this was the keeper.

I highly suggest reading all five parts of this book in order – in the same way that you first go to grade school, then to high school, and finally to college. As much as sex seems like the enticing part, you can't go to college until you have graduated from the prerequisite training. Following the series in this way builds to a much deeper understanding of how sex relates to building your own life and relationship. With the enhancement of letting Spirit be your guide and intuition direct you in what you need to do next, you will naturally progress through the stages that build greater intimacy and love in both your relationship and in your sex life.

Introduction to "HE♥RTGASM!"

Two surprisingly related trends in relationship books, make up the basis of "HE♥RTGASM! – Increasing Intimacy & Ecstasy with Your Beloved."©

One trend is realizing that men and women truly are different, even though they may both strive to be equal. Interestingly enough, the material in this book applies not only to the more obvious heterosexual couples, but to same-sex couples as well, especially when realizing that men and women have a combination of masculine and feminine energies as part of their physical and psychological makeup.

Regardless of the type of relationship, couples find it very difficult to resolve their differences, and if it weren't for coming together to create the synergy of a higher purpose, they could become part of the sad statistic that 50% of marriages end in divorce. Realizing a higher purpose highlights the second trend, a progression towards incorporating spiritual concepts into everyday living.

More than smoothing out the wrinkles, the realizations coming from being able to surrender to the highest good, saves tons of work on eliminating power struggles. Breaking free from cultural myths and old-paradigm thinking helps bring people the freedom they long for. This is the easy and effortless approach to freedom and allows partners and singles to both get what they want as individuals, and as a couple – a "Soul Couple," one might say, "...making their way along their combined soul's journeys."

In ever-expanding areas of life, we are seeing worldwide, that higher consciousness is appearing everywhere. People are ready for conscious partnership based on the radiant energy exchange accessible through a sacred relationship.

"HE♥RTGASM! – Increasing Intimacy & Ecstasy with Your Beloved"© is about attaining conscious partnership through the best of contemporary techniques, set against the background of spiritual concepts based on the ancient sacred Tantric lifestyle. These concepts are most characterized by being heart-centered, being in the moment, being open, moving with the energy, and holding sex as a gift. It's about time for sex to evolve to the next level – to one of conscious partnership.

Getting beyond the social convention of blaming the other person, those who have finally come to the realization that their failed relationships just might have something to do with themselves, will be drawn to search further in this book for the gold it has to offer. It will also appeal to younger people wanting to be in a relationship but don't know how to find a partner and haven't a clue it has something to do with themselves.

PARTICIPANTS WILL LEARN:

- How to set your relationship on FIRE if it has lost its luster

- How partners can take back their individual power and consequently be showered with love and respect from each other.

- How to regain your confidence and feel good about your self

- How a woman can come from her feminine juiciness, and a man can use his focused attention, to bring sex to whole new levels of ecstasy.

- And perhaps most importantly, learn how to successfully deal with relationship problems by using advanced communication techniques based on spiritual concepts, creating a mutual desire to strive for the highest possible good.

High Profile People with a Thumbs-up for Heartgasm!

In revealing her 5 practical secrets "to light your relationship on fire, Toni De Marco candidly shares her personal journey from failed partnerships to relationship success, illustrating how the principals in "HE♥RTGASM!" can take your relationship to the next level of fulfillment. The power and persuasion of her universally time-tested formula for love is so juicy that we can't wait to apply her ideas in our own lives. And it makes you want to be young again. I love this book!

Larry King
TV Personality

"HE♥RTGASM!" integrates the latest in Western psychology with the most practical Eastern spiritual healing modalities. The goal of "HE♥RTGASM!" is bringing these two worlds together to provide people opportunities for healing and transforming their relationships.

In the new millennium we're looking at a world in which health, wholeness and the holy is really all part of the same continuum. Healthy environments, relationships, emotions, and body make up the holistic approach that is needed to reclaim our humanity. You can't have a balanced relationship without every aspect of life being all-inclusive.

At this time, we can all benefit by reawakening our ancient memory of wholeness and tuning-in to more natural methods of experiencing relationships following the lead of Toni De Marco in her new book, "HE♥RTGASM!"

This book is amazingly simple to use and can help both couples and singles on their journey, to find increased intimacy and spiritual meaning in their relationships. It's a great message which needs to be heard!"

Michael Butler

Producer best known for world famous hit musical HAIR

"HE♥RTGASM!" is a much-needed down-to-earth, spirit-centered guide to true intimacy in a relationship. Author, Toni De Marco, presents a cornucopia of spiritual principles and new-paradigm ideas, along with her own experience, in skillfully guiding one's union from relationship hell into relationship heaven in record time. I highly recommend "HE♥RTGASM!" to those who want to learn practical skills that can be used immediately to enhance and improve their lives and intimate relationships.

Robert G. Allen

Best-selling author of Nothing Down, Creating Wealth, Multiple Streams of Income and The One Minute Millionaire

About The Author

Toni De Marco is an internationally renowned seminar leader, speaker, producer, and the author of three books including "HE♥RTGASM! – Increasing Intimacy & Ecstasy with Your Beloved."© Toni has an extensive background in psychology, metaphysics, and health, and is the founder of the Wellness Healing Center. She was originally an actress and cover girl of 'Super Model' fame who went on to writing and producing video and television. TV show guest appearances and/or features include ABC's "Good Morning America," CBS's "Morning Show," the "Sally Show," Regis Philbin's "The Regis & Kathy Show," ESPN's "Business Times," and 55 episodes of "Making a Difference," the latter three of which she also produced. She recently produced a DVD, "Tantric Partner Yoga," as a tool to help couples develop more intimacy in their relationships.

As the host and producer of the above-mentioned TV talk show series for over 4 years, Toni had the opportunity to interview many celebrities, including her favorite, Dr. Deepak Chopra, because, in her words, "Not only is he brilliant, but knows how to speak in sound bites." Some of her other outstanding interviews are of Fritjof Capra, Dr. Bernie Siegel,

Lindsay Wagner, Jon Voight, Kennie Loggins, JP DeJoria, Olivia Newton John, and Archbishop Desmond Tutu.

A Unique Perspective on Fulfilling Relationships Including Great Sex

Toni De Marco has a fresh and unique perspective on relationships and sex.

Most of the conscientious books on relationship never cover the sexual aspects, which she finds hard to comprehend, "Great relationships are *supposed* to have fabulous sex!"

By the way, 'sex' is a word that she equates with 'sensual.' Part of what "HE♥RTGASM!" is about is getting to the ecstasy that is beyond the 15 minutes it takes the average couple to have sex.

She says that, "It isn't until a person can identify or 'merge' with their higher selves, that they can get to higher levels of orgasmic euphoria. Merging with the Divine can instantly remove the veil of Maya separating man and God, activating self-realization and enlightenment." [1] She continues, "It is *because* Tantra is spiritual that you get a whole new perspective of what 'wildly fulfilling' sex can be. In order to go there consistently in a relationship, it helps to learn to relate because it's hard to have sex with a partner you aren't talking to, and to learn to love – especially yourself."

---

1   Maya (Sanskrit), in Indian religions, has multiple meanings, usually quoted as "illusion", centered on the fact that we do not experience the environment itself but rather a projection of it, created by us. Māyā is the principal deity that manifests, perpetuates and governs the illusion and dream of duality in the phenomenal Universe.

Secret 1:

Healing with Communication &
Creating Intimacy by Enhancing
Your Heart Connection

Chapter 1
Trust That the Heart Knows What to Say

Love Is the Greatest Healer of All

H.E.A.R.T. System

Five Secrets – Five parts

Sometimes it seems like just yesterday that I was lying in my bathtub with tears streaming down my face, "I don't understand why he won't talk to me about sex. I *can't stand* not having sex for months at a time – it just doesn't work for me. I wish there was something I could do about it."

But nothing I'd tried seemed to work. Every day I would sit in my bathtub and cry.

Even though my husband and I owned a beautiful Mediterranean villa overlooking the Hollywood Hills and had a Mercedes and a Porsche in the garage, I was desperately unhappy.

That's when I realized that money and fame were empty and meaningless without being satisfied with my inner-self and my relationship.

Practically virgins when we married, we just didn't know enough about sex to make it work. He kept telling me I was I was frigid. I didn't feel frigid but I didn't have orgasms either and was beginning to believe him.

We broke up for a period of time and I went away and had an affair. For me it was a wonderful healing because I realized that I was fully orgasmic and there was nothing wrong with me.

Thus began a new phase of my life in which I spent a great deal of time trying to fix my relationship, fix myself, and learn more about the spiritual side of life. And somewhere along that path I decided that realizing enlightenment in this lifetime had become part of the process.

My husband and I actually had a very close connection because we had so much love for each other. We did everything together, and if we had a break from work, we even had lunch together. We had similar interests and similar tastes in art. If we'd been able to resolve our sexual issues we might still have been together.

So why couldn't we resolve our sexual issues?

We were used to communicating on a very shallow level. We didn't have the skills or tools to communicate about relationship issues. If we'd had that, along with the love we already felt for each other, we might have been able to make things work.

That's why the first section of this book, Secret 1, has been designed specifically to help you to resolve your relationship problems through improving your communication skills – skills specific to opening your heart.

Once you have the tools for expressing your feelings, and asking your partner for what you would prefer, you will even find that you can communicate better sexually. In these ways you can create more intimacy and enhance and expand your heart connection.

By going through each of the five secrets in the order in which they're presented, you'll gain knowledge and understanding that leads to building the intimacy and love that you seek.

Relating Through Love

Through "HE♥RTGASM!," you will gain the knowing that there *is* a way to have a great relationship *and* fabulous sex by acknowledging your own sacred hearts and lives in partnership with your *significant* other.

Essential in a great relationship is to be introduced to your own *inner* Sacred Relationship. Through learning to listen to the intuition of your heart, and finding the love within, loving yourself becomes possible. This is the fast track to rise above the power struggles of a relationship devoid of spirit and finding truly unconditional love for your partner.

You will come to understand that love is the greatest healer there is. It can truly liberate your heart and soul, helping you to soar beyond petty differences, and instead, allowing you to appreciate your individuality, free your creativity, and re-create your world in a new paradigm of how real freedom can look.

You'll discover that by reversing the long-ignored feminine intuitive process, in both men and women, you can add measurably to the way that both partners can experience equality, at the same time playing on the beautiful and obvious differences between the sexes.

Becoming a Soul Couple

Perhaps most importantly, through practicing the advanced communication skills in "HE♥RTGASM!," you can truly become a "soul couple," where you and your partner agree to going for the higher, greatest good – allowing you to safely negotiate for what you both want as individuals, and as a couple – actually getting what you want!

And just in case you think that this book is just for couples, it isn't. Even if you don't have a partner, what you learn will help you to avoid the pitfalls of an uninformed relationship, and actually help you attract the right partner.

Both singles and couples can participate in experiential processes that are fun and rewarding. You'll learn techniques in how to ask for what you want, especially in how you would like to be touched, thus leading to greater appreciation, intimacy and a genuinely loving relationship.

There is also a juicy section devoted just to sensual techniques – always performed in alignment with our Higher Selves, which can actually bring you to experiencing enlightenment.

The Evolution of My Own Life Became The H.E.A.R.T. System

In revealing my five simple and practical secrets to light your relationship on fire, I share with you my personal journey from failed partnerships to relationship success, illustrating how the principals in "HE♥RTGASM!" can take your sacred union to the next level of fulfillment.

These five secrets are really simple and are guaranteed perk up your relationship, however, depending on where you are starting, they may or may not be easy. Nonetheless, I promise you, that if you practice each of these secrets in the order that they are presented, it won't take you long to have a growing and thriving partnership.

My Steps Along the Way

Having been in the public eye for years, I am well-positioned and finally experienced and wise enough, to be the spokesperson who nurtures people into taking this leap into higher consciousness. My career as a relationship guru evolved out of my own experiences, starting out with five years of scholarship-awarded university studies, evolving to becoming a well-known cover girl, and eventually actress, author, and producer. Getting here was not always easy nor was it always a straight path.

Growing Up

When I was very young, it was *supposed* to work like this: Your knight in shining armor sweeps you up on his stallion and together you ride off into the sunset and live happily ever after.

But by the time I was seven, I had developed this nagging suspicion that maybe things wouldn't be so perfect after all. By then I had decided that my parents were full of s**t and that grownups couldn't be trusted.

Still, I had hope. All those romantic novels I had read in my teen years couldn't have been wrong, could they? They depicted lovers having this beautiful spiritual bonding, holding them together regardless of the problems which beset them, and which in fact, cemented the love between them even greater than before. But as you will see in the upcoming chapters of this book, that's not the way it turned out.

My life's path to find my dream of spiritual partnership grew out of my need to fix my parents, and therefore to fix my relationships and myself.

Thus commenced my life-long search to understand what makes people tick, which is probably one of the reasons I initially decided to become an actress. From the time of about age 18 on, I launched into an intense study of everything holistic I could get my hands on. Over the last 40 years my background has grown to include an extensive knowledge of psychology, physiology, spirituality, and metaphysics.

Connecting from the Intelligence of the Heart

Trust That the Heart Knows What to Say

Perhaps people start out their relationship-life all backwards – I certainly did. First they have sex, then they fall in love, and then they realize that they can't talk to each other. Chances are if you're not talking, you're not having sex. That's why in "HE♥RTGASM!," I propose you first learn how to relate, and then how to love (especially how to love yourself) – both of which finally enhance your sex life. Not that you can't do it the other way, but you'd better have relationship-tools as a back up when the honeymoon is over.

How would you like to be able to have a perfect intimate relationship in which you have loving ecstatic sex? In everyone's heart of hearts, this is their deepest desire.

In modern cultures, the desire of a man to become wealthy is often behind wanting to attract the perfect wife. Conversely, a woman's desire to be beautiful is often to attract the perfect husband. Dr. Hyla Cass says "This is biologically built in: Men want beautiful women – healthy child-bearers, for reproduction; women want wealthy men who can go out and hunt and bring home the buffalo…so we have to deal with some biological realities…"

Like in David Byrne's lyrics, "Once in a Lifetime," people work all their lives to achieve their dreams and wake up one day with the realization that the life they've created – with the perfect wife, house, and car – isn't what they really wanted after all, and they can't compute how they've allowed this to happen.

This book was created to help people to find themselves through their hearts, to learn to relate to their loved ones through their hearts (and whether married or single), to transform their relationships into heaven on earth.

Welcome to this journey to finding yourself – and in so doing, finding all that you desire.

Hands on Heart & Other Processes

So much of a modern couple's day starts out with a BANG. Jump out of bed, shower, dress, gulp coffee, out the door to work. If you have kids, you can also squeeze that into this litany. Too tired or wired when you get home to do anything  but the essentials? Prepping a meal, corralling the kids to eat, chilling out with a beer and TV dinner in the living room, crawl into bed after the TV puts you to sleep? When do you ever have a chance to get a little intimacy, much less have a chance to make love when you both are so incredibility busy? Hopefully "He♥rtgasm!" will provide the antidote to the problems that arise out of a hectic lifestyle that is now considered normal.

One of the most important things a couple can do to get started in establishing intimacy is just connecting more physically. That quick peck on the cheek as you run out the door isn't really going to do the job.

That's why I start with the "Hands on Heart" process. This will give you a quick start in connecting with your beloved (or re-connecting as the case may be) anytime during the day – especially before you get out of bed in the morning, perhaps when you get home at night, and/or hopefully at night before you fall asleep.

At the beginning or the end of your day, you can get more connected and intimate with your partner by doing a 1 to 3 minute "Hands on Heart Process." You simply connect at your heart centers, synchronizing your breathing, and sending your heart energy around in a big circle from your heart to your beloved's heart and back. It feels so satisfying when you are doing this – it heightens your feelings of love for each other, and gives you a warm start that lingers with you all day long. Of course you will end this process with a big melting hug (see pg. 63)

At the end of this chapter is a description of exactly how to do this process. Once you've done it a few times, you can make up your own modified versions. For example, if you are in a hurry and just running out the door, one modification you could try, that would only take 30 seconds, is instead of sitting facing each other, to do a "quickie" version of the process standing up.

Throughout this book, there are other processes at the end of most chapters that I suggest you implement as close to the time you read about them as possible. You will start to reap the benefits offered immediately so don't wait too long. Often I suggest doing a process with someone other than your beloved, so you can practice first, and bring it freshly to your partner when you've gotten it down so that he/she will be more receptive when they try it with you.

Toni De Marco

Your Cherished Union CAN Be Heaven on Earth

Your Heart's Unspoken Desire: Finding Relationship Heaven

What does having heaven in your relationship mean to you? What does it look like? How many times a day do you say "If only it were this way?" "If only it were that way?" "Things would be so much better if...."

So much of what I used to wish for in my early relationships had to do with "If only the other person would...." "If only my mate were this way or that way."

It was a surprise to me to find out that it was probably not the other person that had to change, but myself.

I didn't think I asked for the life I was getting, but according to the "Law of Attraction," on some level I did. I found out that life doesn't just "happen to you" – you beam it in, exactly according to your expectations and patterns.

John Lennon noticed that life is what happens when you're busy making other plans. I wonder if he learned, as I did, that life is a reflection of our deepest sub-conscious thoughts through the law of attraction.

You might call the law of attraction the ABC's of quantum physics, and according to this law, the vibration that emanates from you attracts or brings in, a similar or complimentary vibration. So what I was beaming out from myself is what I ended up attracting.

This is why the person I needed to change was *me!* What I learned from my first metaphysical teachers, Joel and

Dr. Champion Teutsch, is that if you change yourself, then your partner will shift accordingly. Abraham-Hicks, another metaphysical teacher, calls this finding a vibrational match. The energy we emit from our inner core can be perceived as a vibration and like-vibrations attract.

By stepping out of the little box in which I had lived my life, I could begin to see that, although the universe is infinite, like an infinity ribbon, it always comes back around to its origin. Whether I thought this was fair or not, the universe was always bringing analogous people, situations, things, and a life that I had "vibrationally" asked for, back into my field.

Unless you are making conscious shifts in your thinking and perceptions, you may not feel you are in control of your own life. I definitely did not feel in control.

It was a hard lesson for me to adsorb, that when you consciously shift your vibrational field, the people around you must shift or split away. Why? If that shift feels too uncomfortable for your partner (because their patterns will necessarily have to change to reflect your new vibration), that person may not be enough in "resonance" with you, and will have no choice but to go a different direction. It was through my two back-to-back marriages that I got this realization big time.

Toni De Marco

My Two Completely Different Husbands and How They're Being Around Me Turned Them Into Raging Maniacs

In my first marriage, I used to cry myself to sleep at night because the little amount of sex we had in the beginning of our relationship had dwindled down to nothing. The last vestiges of communication fluctuated between being ignored and being verbally abused. Eventually, no sex was the outcome of no communication.

Interestingly enough, my second marriage, even though my next husband was completely different, turned out almost exactly like the first one. I had the realization that if I had the same outcome from both 7-year marriages, that it probably was not about them, but something about me that attracted the same outcome. What signal or vibration was I putting out to be treated like this – to be put down, verbally abused, and not heard?

Hmmm, this sounded familiar – so it wasn't too hard to figure out. By that time I'd had years of studying with my mentors, the Teutsches, and knew that almost all negative patterns come from our parents.

There was no doubt that since my father treated me like this, (put me down, verbally abused me, and wouldn't listen to what I had to say) that I had attracted men who loved me so much that they gave me exactly what I was unconsciously asking for. How scary was that?

14

Process Reviews and Exercises

Hands on Heart Process

The first process I encourage readers to do, is to find a partner, whether it be a friend or a lover, who you can learn to connect with at your heart center. This helps get you right into the basic premise of relating from the heart. If no one is available, do it with yourself, sitting cross-legged in front of a mirror.

Since my "Hands on Heart" process can be done with a friend or lover, it's not about sex. It can even be done with two same-sex people. It's about connecting body, soul, and heart. This instant connection shows that we are all made of the same stuff – we are all the same inside.

- The couple sits facing each other either knee-to-knee or closer if desired, like in the Yab-Yum[2] position, where the man sits cross-legged and the woman sits on his lap and wraps her legs around his waist. You can also sit cross-legged in front of each other. Just make sure you are able to reach your partner's heart with your right hand and vice-versa. Your left hand covers your partner's right hand on your heart and vice-versa. Initially, close your eyes and feel your partner's heart beat (this might take a minute or two).

- Then imagine that the colors and energy patterns you see behind your closed eyes is the result of your combined heart energies. You might even describe to each other what colors you are seeing. For example, people often see darks and purples, somewhat interspersed with the energetic movement of subdued pinks, golds, and whites. There is no right or wrong in this, only that you use your imagination to describe the heart energies you are feeling between the two of you.

- Next, without moving your hands, open your eyes and gaze into your partner's eyes. Since the left eye represents the feminine or receptive side, it

2 Yab-Yum (Tibetan literally, "father-mother") is a common symbol in the Buddhist art of India, Bhutan, Nepal, and Tibet representing the male deity in sexual union with his female consort. Often the male deity is sitting in lotus position while his consort is sitting in his lap. Taken more lightly, Tantrikas sometimes refer to it as the "Yum-Yum" position.

is even more effective to gaze into each other's left eye. This may be a bit uncomfortable at first, because people are not usually so direct. But stay with it and imagine that you are looking directly into their soul. You can imagine a bright white or golden light deep down inside and see their magnificence, their warm love, and the beauty that we all are inside, and then tell your partner what you see.

• Next you might want to do the Namaste Greeting. Holding hands up in a prayer position, hands intertwined if desired, come close enough now to almost be touching foreheads and repeat the following together: "The Divine in me, recognizes, and honors, the Divine in You – Namaste." On saying Namaste, bow slightly to touch foreheads, and notice that your partner's two eyes have merged into one – symbolic of the one we all are. Give your partner (or yourself) a nice hug, and then slowly separate and move apart.

What is Tantric Energy?

Why is "sexual energy" not talked about in the West? And what is Tantric Energy? Please write your impressions of what these energies mean to you before you read further.

We will go into more depth about this in later chapters but keep your notes on this and be thinking about how Tantric Energy might be different than or part of sexual energy.

Chapter 2
You Can't Make Love Until You Make Peace

Your Heart Knows What You Want

How is "Making Love" different than sex?

Making love is intimate and requires opening your heart to loving your partner – sex is sex.

Let's expand this definition and talk about sex combined with making love.

Before Making Love, Clear up the Past

How can you make love to a partner you're not getting along with? Can you make love if you aren't talking to each other? How do you get "off" upsets?

What do you do when one person wants sex and the other doesn't?

In this chapter, you'll be introduced to many tools that will help you to communicate better. It is only when you can talk together peaceably that the relationship will expand, grow, and give you the loving intimacy you so desire. In this way the two of you can become greater than either one of you individually, and still both retaining your unique individuality.

My First Marriage

Let's go back to that time when I was desperately unhappy and spent hours in the bathtub, gazing out over the valley below, wondering if I would ever be happy again, and not knowing how to tell my husband what was wrong. He didn't seem to want to listen to me about sex. He had heard it all before and he just didn't want to go there. What could I do to make him change?

Now, many years later, I realize that I was fixated on how I could change him, not about what I could change about myself. It has taken me many years to realize that you can never make anyone change. I used to think that I could use positive thinking to change my partner.

Since everyone has free will, your partner has to decide they *want* to change. In fact, the more you push against someone, the more likely they will resist change.

The only way you can influence another to change is to *be* the change you want to see in them. By being and acting who you hope others would be, they can see how well it works for you and decide to go there with you. On the other hand, because you are both now operating on different vibrational levels, the other person might well decide to go elsewhere – it's entirely up to them.

In romantic relationships, chances are, that you both fantasized that the other person had qualities you imposed on them, and only later, when the initial feelings of euphoria had faded away, realize that you barely know that person, and often, that you wish you *didn't* know that person as well as you do now.

What to do? A relationship can only work if both people are ready, willing and able to change, or at least be willing to talk about why things aren't working. Willing communication is the key to most of what you will learn in this book.

At some point, you may realize that you really *don't* belong with this person, because there is just no opening for negotiation. If it's "my way or the highway," maybe it *is* time to move on. The Irish Catholic family pattern in the era when my parents got together was, that women don't have a say. When my dad made a decision, that was it – it became the rule. My mom was expected to obey his every edict. Hopefully we've come a long way since those days, but many families still operate from this old paradigm.

It is not really satisfying for either person. Ideally, both people in a relationship are equal. Only then can a relationship grow to heights of ecstasy beyond what gender-restricted relationships offer. This is not to say that women and men aren't different – just equal in their rights as human beings.

If, at any point in this process, you reach an impasse with your partner, try to process through the problem with the materials offered in this book.

Remember, this won't work if only *one* of you wants to do it. You *both* have to be willing to look at the problems and be willing to make some changes. Both of you have to take 100% responsibility because the law of attraction is operating at all levels of your life. You can't go searching on the outside for what's wrong. You might ask yourself, "What signal is it that I'm putting out to attract the abuse I'm receiving?"

"Am I taking responsibility for what's coming my way, especially from my partner?" It's only when you take 100% responsibility for your own life that things can change.

Do you know what the definition of insanity is? It's when you keep doing things the same way expecting different results.

Forgiveness – Severing the Ugly Cords Binding the Past to Your Present

Forgiving the Unforgivable Requires Opening Your Heart to Yourself

Forgiveness is prime among the things you can do to clear a space in your consciousness and get on with your life. Mental garbage clutters up our mental space and makes it hard to think clearly. I once took a course in energy healing and through visualizing what "thoughts" might look like if you could see them, we became familiar with "thought forms." I soon started to think of negative thought forms as dark little boxes of energy floating around in one's aura. A really practiced psychic practitioner can actually see these thought forms.

Have you and your partner cleared a space for the possibility of sex, or are you still mad at each other? Chances are, a couple's being mad at each other starts with being so adamant that *you* are right. So much so in fact, that you must make the other person wrong. With this attitude, there is no space for forgiveness or negotiation.

Learning more about forgiveness is just the beginning of a process where you will begin to see that it is not the other person, but you that you are not forgiving. Once you can begin to forgive your self, you will soon see that not forgiving the other person is just holding you back from a happy and fulfilling life.

The Buddha on Forgiveness

"Resentment is the kind of anger that you carry around for a long time. It is like a hot coal that you pick up and intend to throw at somebody else, but the whole time it is burning you. We give up a lot of energy by holding on."

Here is a good example of not being able to forgive: Almost everybody has some relative that did something so horrendous to them, that they will never, ever forgive them. Unfortunately, this gives deceased relatives the power to continue hurting us all our lives, even though those people may have been dead for 20 years.

Anna's Forgiveness Breakthrough

At a workshop I facilitated in Mullumbimby (a little village near Byron Bay), Australia, there was a woman, Anna, who was unable to forgive her whole community, including her mother and entire family. They were holding something against her for which she did not feel responsible. She felt she was completely right, and all the rest of them were completely wrong in unfairly judging her.

When asked how heavy a weight this was to carry around, you could see just by her body language that it was unbearably heavy. She said this had ruined her life, and even though she had long left this place behind, on being questioned, she admitted that she dragged it along behind her everywhere she went.

"What if you could forgive your community," I posited, "and you could let go of this old baggage you are dragging around? You know, you are not hurting *them* by being unforgiving. It is you, *yourself,* that you are hurting. How much more hurt and pain are you willing to keep submitting yourself to?"

She then flew into a rage, which very soon broke down into a flood of tears, all the while sobbing, "I cannot forgive them! What they have done to my reputation and to me is un-forgivable."

I held her while she continued sobbing, reminding her that it was her choice to give it up – that she could keep holding on to it as long as she wanted to.

After a few minutes, she sat up and dried her tears and announced, "You are right. I don't want to feel like this any more. I don't want to forgive them, but I will."

"And who else are you willing to forgive?" She immediately knew it was herself that she also had to forgive.

At that point I guided the entire group through the "forgiveness process," which I had the young lady in question read out loud. Please find this process a few paragraphs below. Nothing could have more clearly demonstrated the forgiveness process, than what the entire group had not only witnessed, but participated in, just by holding the space for this amazing breakthrough to happen.

I think we can all now agree with Mother Theresa who said, "We know that if we really want to love we must learn to forgive."

Mother Teresa of Calcutta at a pro-life meeting in 1986 in Bonn, *Germany.*
Photo Túrelio (via Wikimedia-Commons), Creative Commons BY-SA 2.0-de

Who is it that you have to forgive? Is it un-forgivable? Why?

Getting out paper and pen again, write what & whom you consider "unforgivable." An example of something you might write could be,

"I can't forgive my mother for what she did to me."

Why is being right more important than "getting off it" and getting on with your life? When are you going to be so sick and tired of dragging your old baggage around that you are willing to give it up?

Once you have determined who in your own life you need to forgive the most, I suggest going through the whole following process, part of which is forgiving yourself. Then continue to do this process every day for the next week, or as often as is necessary, to let go of the old baggage of "un-forgiveness" you are dragging behind you everywhere you go:

The Forgiveness Process

I now choose...of my own free will...to forgive you...for everything that has occurred between us...in this life... and in any lifetime...through all time and space...So be it. Breathe in and release.

I now ask that you forgive me...for whatever I have said or done...whether conscious or unconscious...in this or any other life...or plane of existence. Please forgive me, please forgive me...please forgive me...now. Through the grace of God...So be it.

Breathe in and release.

I now choose to forgive myself...for my lack of skillfulness...for causing us pain and heartache...I am truly sorry. May I be forgiven...through the grace of God...So be it.

Breathe in and release.

I ask that all cords of attachment...that bind us to pain...be released. May these be cut...and set free...Through all lifetimes...and all dimensions... Now. Through the grace of God... So be it. Breathe in, raise your hand and CUT through the imaginary cords of attachment going outwards from your belly-button. *[You might ask Archangel Michael to use his powerful flaming sword to help you to cut through the cords of attachment]* Release.

I set you free...fully and completely. I ask that you be blessed...with every happiness and joy...through the grace of God...so be it. Breathe in and release.

I now release all of your energy...that I have been carrying for you..from my body...mind..and energy field. I return this to you...Now. Breathe in and release.

I call back my spirit...from all of the people ...places ...things ...times ...and events...that we have shared... and I call back my energy and spirit... from...you now. With gratitude and love, and thanks for all that you have taught me...so be it.

Breathe in and hold, and breathe normally.

Say – **"I choose to forgive myself for all of the mistakes that I have ever made, for failing to love and for my**

difficulty with forgiving, I forgive myself through all time and space. Through the grace of God, so be it."

Blessings:

I am a child of Goddess/God. I am worthy of all good things. I choose to love myself and to develop compassion and love for all. I am that I am. So be it. Breathe in and hold, and then breathe normally.

Dismantling Bastions of Unconscious Patterns, Expectations, and Beliefs

Are Your Unconscious Patterns Running You? If Your Patterns Aren't Running You, You have a Chance of Running Yourself

Have you ever noticed that there are "patterns" that keep repeating over and over in your life? For example, have you gotten rid of one partner, only to find that the next one does the same things you hated about the previous one – or even worse?

This happened to me – one partner after another had continued to verbally abuse me, and sometimes, even physically hurt me. At some point I had to admit that I had kept partnering with my "dad" – not the actual one of course, but no matter how different they appeared to be at first, if they weren't like my dad at all, I would turn then into my dad. I was really horrified to have made this realization. I stayed away from intimate relationships for years as a result.

Ninety Percent of Getting Rid of a Problem Is Realizing That You Have One

My first success-consciousness coach, Dr. Champion Teutsch, used to say "Ninety percent of getting rid of a problem is realizing that you have one."

You can start with seeing "out there," as what is being reflected back to you. If you don't like it, contemplate what part of the problem is being caused by you.

Most people don't want to take the responsibility of claiming their part in what's going wrong. Usually "it's *their* fault," they say, pointing a finger at someone else. Pointing fingers is risky business – if you look at where your other fingers are while you're pointing, 3 are pointing back at you!

Blaming and shaming is very low on the totem pole of human "beingness," on a scale ranging from negative to positive. According to Dr. David Hawkins[3] in his "Scale of Consciousness" chart from his insightful book, "Power vs. Force," 'blame and shame' are the two most negative emotions on the scale.

This may be hard to get at first, but you can never change your circumstances until you are ready to accept your responsibility for what you see and experience in the world.

---

3   More on Hawkins on page 87 including footnote on page 88.

You may already be aware of how you need to take responsibility in everything that happens in your life. If you can remember, write down your first "ah-ha" about this metaphysical law – the law of attraction – i.e., the realization that what you put out on a vibrational level is always what you get back, in some form or another.

In the end, the truth is that one must accept 100% responsibility for all of it.

Discovering Your Attachment to Old Negative Patterns Can Bring About Life Changing Transformations

How a Man Changed His Co-dependent Relationship with His Mother

[Note: If this story triggers any of your own patterns or feelings, you might want to jot down a few notes during this process]

I'll never forget the man who said I changed his life: Leo came running down the hall at "The Spa" where he was taking my workshop and said, "I just want to thank you for changing my life!"

"As far back as I can remember, I have awakened angry every day of my life, and since we did that process in class, every day for the last 3 days I have awakened happy. That whole anger thing is just gone."

Basically, he was angry with his Mother because she was so controlling. She just couldn't say anything nice about anything he did in his life – she always had to spoil everything by negating it.

When he told his mom he was getting married to a Thai woman, she would have nothing of it. None-the-less, she flew from the US to Thailand to attend the wedding.

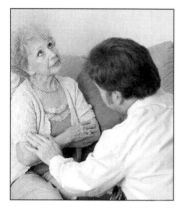

The icing on the cake (so to speak) happened on the day he married his lovely Thai girlfriend. With the three of them in a limo on the way to their reception, his mother, with no regards for his new wife being in clear earshot, said, "I don't know why you had to go and marry a foreigner."

That made him so angry that he wanted to throttle her but he was so embarrassed that he didn't say anything. The atmosphere in the car was already so heavy you could cut it with a knife. So he just smoldered, thinking "Why does she have to put a damper on a perfectly lovely and happy wedding? She does it every time."

This was totally consistent with the fact that his mom could never, ever, say anything nice about him or praise him, and once again he was totally chagrined.

Even though that made him feel helpless, in my workshop, he was **still brave enough** to speak up and let us know the depth of his pain.

The process we did with him in this class involved everyone in the room, and because he was brave enough to talk about it, he was able to go for the gold. The end result being that he realized, because he was not his mom, that what she did and who she was, was not a reflection on him. He could be his own person. He was able to break this co-dependent pattern with his mom through the realization that it wasn't about him and that he didn't have to play this game any more.

One of the points we touched on is that he is a spiritual being in a human body. This gave him more perspective on his higher or bigger self, rather than the little self, so besot with destructive mental patterns that there seemed to be no way out of, until this moment.

He was able to forgive her – not that he really wanted to, but because he knew that it would continue to ruin his life if he didn't. So he forgave her and let her go.

What an amazing transformation!

What other transformations happened in his life because of these results?

He and his wife are happily married with a 3-year-old daughter and no matter what his mother thinks, he is just fine without her opinion.

What would the cost have been to Leo had he **not** accepted the offer to be in my workshop?

He would have continued in his life being unhappy, and his wife would probably be unhappy too. They may have succumbed to the statistic that 1 out of every two marriages ends in divorce.

When you've read this book and done the exercises in the *"Process Reviews and Exercises"* sections at the end of many chapters, you too, may realize you can turn your life around. It only takes an instant of realization!

Family patterns going back, sometimes for endless generations, are what make up most of what we are. We are not really who we think we are if we are just living out other people's patterns, are we?

The more we fight against becoming what we hate, the more we become it.

How do we get out of this endless chain of abuse? We take responsibility. We realize that we have attracted these people in our lives in order to heal ourselves, perhaps to heal our parents, and to break away from these patterns.

Bigger Gratitude – Greater Progress

Along the lines of pursuing the meaning of the law of attraction, let's talk about the benefits of being grateful, appreciative, and giving thanks whenever possible.

Do you have friends that complain all the time? Do *you* complain all the time – even to yourself? What kind of body language accompanies bitching and moaning, or thinking, "Why did this have to happen to me?" A bent over body and a shuffling gait is a sure sign that you need to pull yourself up out of the doldrums and into an attitude of gratitude.

One the other hand, think of something you are grateful for. Notice how just thinking about being grateful makes you sit up straighter in your chair and puts a smile on your face.

No Bitchin' n Moanin'

In Edwene Gaines' book, "The Four Spiritual Laws of Prosperity," she offers a process she calls the "21 Day

Challenge." Edwene says, "If you can do *anything* for 21 days, it will become a part of your very soul." So, like her, I made the commitment that for 21 days I would not gossip, criticize, complain to others or myself, or use any negative language.

When I started the challenge, I put a sticky note on my fridge, starting with today's date, with check boxes for the next 21 days. Each day that I could go without being negative, a check would go into the box. If I screwed up, I would start over again for another whole 21 days. I started over again and again every 2 or 3 days until I became so super conscious of my thoughts that I made it all the way to day 19, but, because I slipped and gossiped about a friend, I had to start all over again. Doing this really makes you think twice about what you are putting out into the Universe, consciously or unconsciously. I'm very grateful for the heightened awareness this process gave me of my every thought.

Now, when I'm around friends who gossip, complain, and are generally negative, I change the subject to something more uplifting, or if I have to, just leave the room. I often say to someone on a bitch-binge, "I'd rather not talk about 'so-and-so' because gossiping doesn't help – I'd rather not contribute to putting anyone down. Instead I choose to give people the benefit of the doubt, regardless of their behavior." This takes a lot of courage, but works, none-the-less.

If you would like to participate in my world-wide campaign to join the "He♥rtgasm! 21 Day Challenge" please go to the back of this book for more information (Appendix, page 265).

In the appendix, besides an interview with Edwene, I've also I've interviewed Rev. Will Bowen, who took up Edwena's challenge by distributing wristbands creating awareness all over the world that you *can* eradicate complaining from your lives.

We've also made special bracelets/wristbands available as a reminder to keep your thoughts and languaging positive. Wearing the "He♥rtgasm! 21 Day Challenge" bracelet will help you to keep your commitment current until you make it all the way through a whole 21 days without backsliding.

An Attitude of Gratitude

The really great thing that happens by this subtle shift of attitude, is that you are contributing to your own growth. Growing your consciousness *and* looking for the positive in everything is propelling you into greater and better circumstances in your life. All the great spiritual teachers know this secret, which, by the way, you will find in the movie, "The Secret."

Abundance author, Sarah Ban Breathnach says, "You simply will not be the same person two months from now after consciously giving thanks each day for the abundance that exists in your life. And you will have set in motion an ancient spiritual law: the more you have and are grateful for, the more will be given you."

Country music songwriter/performer, Willie Nelson said, "When I started counting my blessings, my whole life turned around."

Mother Teresa was a primary example of focusing on the solution, not the problem. She said, "Never let anyone come to you without coming away better and happier." Her entire life revolved around helping others in need – Just look at the love she generated in her life!

Instead of complaining about what you don't have or what's not working, instead of digging yourself deeper into the hole you may already be in, you can be grateful for what you *do* have. *Then* you will be creating a positive field that will quickly come back to you with surprisingly wonderful results.

What you think about expands, so keep focused on the high side, and keep creating more good, instead of sinking into depression about what's not working.

I make it a practice to be thankful in advance of getting the positive new things I'm affirming and creating in my life. I might say something like, "Thank you so much, Goddess, for sending me all the money I need for my trip to New York. I'm so appreciative that you are always there for me when I most need it."

Statue of the Greek Goddess Aphrodite, also called Venus De Milo

In case you are wondering why I use the word, 'Goddess,' it is just to acknowledge the feminine aspect of my own Divine nature, which is also Source energy. Not to mention the fact that I am referring to an all-pervasive energy that is not a 'being' at all – therefore having no sex. In today's culture there is so much focus on male superiority that I like to shake things up a bit by helping people to focus on the gentler, more sensual and nurturing aspects of our image of "all that is" or whatever you choose to call Source.

I've learned to take time every day to spend a minute or two reflecting on the things, people and events in my life for which I'm grateful. What can *you* be grateful for in your life right now? Try starting a Gratitude Journal. The simplest little things for which you can say "thank you" will start to multiply goodness, and uplift your day.

Now here's the kicker you'd least expect: You can even learn to be grateful for the "bad" things – the tough spots in your life, because they lead you (even if you have to be dragged kicking and screaming) to the lessons you need to learn, which in turn, bring you to a higher level in your spiritual development. When you've gotten through that nasty transition, you now have another thing for which you can be grateful.

So it's a good habit to look for the hidden treasure in something that initially seems unfortunate. It may take some digging, but its well worth it to get you out of the dumps, and back into an attitude of gratitude.

Now is the time to turn over a new leaf: Write someone a thank you note today.

Process Reviews and Exercises

PART 1

If you haven't done so already, go back to page 23 and review the Forgiveness Process. Decide who it is that you have to forgive. Usually the other side of that includes forgiving yourself.

PART 2

Now that you've done the Forgiveness Process, it's a good idea to look more deeply into your relationship life. The following is a "set-up" to bring your consciousness into awareness of when you are blaming others or circumstances for the stuff you don't like in your life.

Once again, write 2 or 3 answers to each the following questions before proceeding.

- What works in my relationships, and what doesn't work?

- What works in "love", and what doesn't work?

- What works in sex, and what doesn't work?

- What are my intended results from reading this book?

If, for example, you have said how badly your partner treats you, and "What they have done to me isn't working," where is it that you have taken responsibility? Many people refuse to believe that they are at least partly responsible for something that someone else has "done to them."

Let's "reframe" this and ask how the quality of your life would change if you were willing to take some responsibility. Or even all of the responsibility? Take a moment to look at what you have written and make this "reframe" to include how you may have contributed to the results that you don't like. How does this make you feel?

Is your righteousness so strong that you can't move from your stance because you don't want to admit that if you *did* create this problem you would have to  forgive them *and* yourself? Now that you know it is *you* who are in control, not the other person or circumstance you are blaming, you can get off the stance of making someone wrong. Which feels better: To remain in a stalemate (which feels terrible), or to get off this position and "try on" feeling better?

PART 3

Now is the time to start thinking about what you are grateful for. Every day this week, first thing when you wake up in the morning, think of all the things for which you can give thanks. And when you have a chance, write down the 10 things for which you are most grateful.

PART 4

If you feel you are ready, start today and accept the "21 Day Challenge" to refrain from gossip, criticism, complaining (to others or even yourself), or the use any negative language.

Chapter 3:

How Both Partners can "Have It Their Way"

The Heart Cares Not for Things — Only For How It Wants to Feel

Conceive the Future of Your Relationship

Not many people who get together in a new partnership talk about their feelings and how they want to feel in the relationship. Ambitions for what they want to achieve, either in business, or in material possessions are usually shared. But because they seldom have positive role models for structuring a relationship around love, compassion, and joy, it's not likely that they get into feelings.

Just sink into your heart for a moment – what does your heart want to feel? Cherished, loved, honored, understood?

The way of the heart would suggest envisioning these qualities for the relationship to continue successfully.

Negotiating a Relationship "Covenant"

Boundaries

It's a good idea to set up boundaries and parameters within which you can "have it your way," at the very *beginning* of the relationship, so there are no surprises later. Let's talk about boundaries.

One of my boundaries that I share with my partner(s) is, "No one talks to me once I'm asleep. Even if I get up to take a leak, I'm still considered to be 'asleep.' It's almost impossible for me to get back to sleep if I have to talk to somebody – even a few words. You'll know that I'm officially 'up,' when I get up and put on clothes, or when I start talking to you first."

Now take this opportunity to write down an example of one of *your* boundaries. Out of this process, you might resolve to talk to your partner about boundaries.

What if the two of you could sit down and hammer out an agreement about honoring each other's boundaries and possibly other agreements you could make about the relationship itself?

Let's call this a "relationship contract." It's not the kind you have to take to an attorney or get notarized, but it's a *real* contract between the two of you about how you agree to relate. I do suggest that both of you sign it.

It's changeable too – it can be renegotiated from time to time as one or both of you realize that parts of it aren't working. In fact, determine a time to review and update your contract, say, once or twice a year (or if needed, on an emergency basis).

Let's come up with some ideas of what you would want in your contract. Perhaps some of your boundaries would go in there. Please get out your notebook and start writing down some of the things you would want in your contract.

Think of setting up boundaries in your contract as a way of saying, "This is who I am and I need to be appreciated even for the ways that you and I are different."

In What Ways Do You Allow Others Into Your Relationship?

What about how the two of you relate around other people? Is it okay for you to go out for a night with the guys or the gals? That's probably fine, but not if you go out every night with friends and leave your partner at home alone.

Would you want your partner to take his or her secretary out to lunch or dinner? When would this be too much?

Do you have an agreement about sexual conduct outside the partnership? If you don't, you should. What if you are monogamous and you find out down the line that your partner isn't, or doesn't want to be? Do you pack up the kids and leave? Maybe it's a good idea to create a "relationship contract" between the two of you *before* you move in with each other, and certainly before you have kids. On the other hand, if you both have an interest in having an open marriage or relationship, this could be refined to the point that it works, as long as you both can be brutally honest.

Are Kids Part of the Plan? – and What About Chores?

Do you both want them? How are they to be raised? Is religion an issue, or *would it be* with children in the picture?

When the honeymoon is over, do household chores become an issue? When started on the right foot, who does what can be worked out so everyone is happy. John Gray[4] says that women should handle the household chores and that men would naturally only be available for emergencies that men so typically can handle like a "Superman coming to the rescue," but I disagree. Today most women have to go to work just like men, so it is totally unfair for a woman to have to bear the brunt of all household responsibilities with just an occasional super-rescue from the man. Here is where you two need to really go into detail about who does what in a way that is fair for both of you. Perhaps the woman might agree to cook and the man does the cleaning up, or vice versa, depending on your skills and attitude towards certain chores.

The two of you will have to hammer out which of the household chores you are each willing to do. Here's where the contract you signed will come in handy. If your partner has agreed to take out the trash and is falling behind, now is the time to pull out the agreement and say, "Look, you agreed to do this and you signed this. So you can't wiggle out now." Of course, it's always an option to renegotiate a more realistic contract if one or the other person feels that something is just not right or is even oppressive.

---

4   John Gray's "Venus on Fire, Mars on Ice: Hormonal Balance - The Key to Life, Love and Energy" (Mind Publishing 2010).

What About Money?

How is money to be shared between you? Do you each have your own bank accounts? Who pays for what? If you have a joint account, are there limits on spending? How do you agree on major expenditures?

There's something to be said for pre-nuptials if one of the partners is bringing most of the money to the table. When my first husband and I split up, by New York State law, we were to split all assets down the middle. At that time, I was willing to go by the law, but looking back on things, I felt that had we negotiated a pre-nuptial agreement, that it would have been more fair for both of us.

It's Never Too Late to Start Now

What if you've already been in a relationship for quite some time now and you never even *thought* of a contract? Perhaps you've been married 10 years and have 2 kids in grade school."

Now is the time to pull all your skeletons out of the closet and talk about them. If that seems too scary at the moment, you might write down to talk to your partner about it later in a scheduled session where you can peacefully talk about issues (more about this later in the section on 'With-holds' sessions).

Should the Kids Always Come First?

Say you already *are* in an established relationship and the two of you are too busy to get together: Both of you have jobs, the kids always *have* to come first – or should they?

If you're not making love enough maybe *you* should come first for a change.

Date Night

Setting up Date Night (with <u>hours</u> of pleasure, not just the usual minutes) is not that hard to do if you plan around it. Pick one consistent night a week that you can spend the whole evening together alone, *without* the kids. Send them out to a babysitter overnight. Or leave them with a baby sitter and go to a motel. Do what ever it takes to keep the sexual energy of your relationship alive.

Role Play Creating a Relationship Contract With a Friend First

Create the opportunity to try out your contract proposal on neutral ears – have a friend role play your partner. Regardless of your friend's gender, they can role-play the sex of your significant other.

Even though they might feel they are different from your partner, be sure to tell the listener doing the role-playing to let their own *real* feelings bubble to the surface and be expressed. You might suggest, "Please be the person *you* are – and don't attempt to say what you *think* my partner would say or would like to hear."

They might feel a relationship contract would actually work, and you need to hear that kind of input. You will learn a lot from this process, and hopefully you can implement it with a friend from time to time.

You or your substitute partner might also conclude, "You know, I thought I would be embarrassed to talk about such intimate stuff with a friend, but it didn't matter in the least. In fact, it was energizing to realize that I can, and do, have a very important say in my contract. I've so appreciated your input."

Compassionate Communication

(aka Non Violent Communication)

What Does Her Heart Want to Feel? – And How About His Heart?

In the heat of an argument how often have your stepped aside and asked yourself, "What does my partner's heart want to feel right now? What does my heart want to feel?" Probably never.

If we can *at least* get to an assessment of our own feelings, and express these to our partner, this can help to by-pass that old circular round-and-round ego-based struggle that leads nowhere.

If you are speaking the truth of how you feel in this particular circumstance, your raging partner will be stopped dead in his/her tracks. "Gosh, honey, I didn't know you felt that way – how come you never told me that before?" might even be the response.

At the very least, your partner can't make you wrong about your feelings – you feel what you feel. At the same you're not making your partner wrong either – just telling the truth in a compassionate way.

Then you might suggest what you would appreciate in place of the way you are currently being treated, just to try it "this one time," as a possibility, not a rule. For example: "I would feel loved and respected if you would ask me what *I* would like to do before you commit to plans for both of us."

The scene I just described is actually following the format for Non-Violent-Communication, NVC, or as it is often called now, Compassionate Communication.

I learned NVC in a course I attended many, many years ago facilitated by Marshall Rosenberg who conceived NVC. Although it was originally used to help to improve family relationships, it has spread world wide, and now The United Nations has adapted NVC as its sole means of arbitrating and establishing peaceful relationships between countries. Partners, couples, and even singles, continue to use this process to communicate compassionately.

When you learn to communicate your feelings, this opens you to discerning your partner's feelings too, thus helping you to becoming more compassionate.

The Basic Format of NVC

NVC has developed and grown so much, that there are courses, workshops and support groups all over the country. There is no *one set way* to start practicing – there are at least 20 or more ways.

Pared down to the bare bones, the following is the simplest format that you can practice with your partner or a friend. The goal is to state your feelings about a problem you are having with someone without trying to make them wrong. To the contrary, you want to treat them with compassion and understanding.

To picture these steps, they are presented in "outline form" in the Process Reviews and Exercises starting, part 3 on page 75.

First it is important to go inside and to identify your feelings about something that is going on with your partner that you are not appreciating.

Once the feeling(s) is identified, this is followed by telling your partner, "When you do (such and such), I feel sad," or angry, disappointment, or whatever it is that you feel.

Remember, that saying "I feel that you are wrong," is not a feeling, but if you are used to "stuffing" your feelings, then it might be more difficult to find them. But they are there, nonetheless, and with practice, you will be able to find them. When practicing with a friend, ask them to help you to identify your feelings if you are having trouble.

Now that you have cued your partner that you are launching into the NVC format, he/she will listen a different way.

Next you are going to ask for what your preference is that you would have them do. For example, perhaps you started out, "When you get angry at me for being late, I feel scared and afraid that you might hurt me."

And you might continue:

"So what I would prefer instead, is that you just point to your watch, smile, and go into the living room and wait five minutes for me to be ready. Would you be willing to do that?"

If he/she says "Yes," the next step is to ask them to repeat what they've agreed to.

Often your partner might forget some important part, or twists the meaning into something you didn't say. You point this out and ask them repeat the part(s) that were not quite right.

Repeating things back until they've got it right, could be the "straw that breaks the camel's back," because, like my friend Rama, in the story below, a partner inexperienced in NVC, will often jump to the conclusion that they are having to eat crow "by rubbing their face in it" especially after they've agreed to try what you've asked for.

If your partner won't agree, at least you can agree to disagree and perhaps discuss it later when you've both had a chance to think about how the two of you can be satisfied with a modified resolution.

In the example above, the problem might be resolved by agreeing to take two cars, so that instead of making them late, they can go ahead without you and you meet them there a bit later.

Dealing with Stubborn or Resistant Partners

In a workshop I did in Bali, one of the participants, Rama, was a handsome 'Latin-lover-type,' who spoke perfect English with a heavy Italian accent. He vehemently disagreed that this would work, *"My girlfriend would NEVER do something like this with me. She would say 'You've got to be joking!' No way would she ever do this. You just don't understand the mentality of these Latin girls!"*

I said, "I think you would be surprised about what some people would do, even if you think they wouldn't. If she got the idea that your relationship might improve, and that she might be able to get what *SHE* wants from it, she might try it."

He still thought it was a crazy idea and over the course of the next couple of hours we practiced the NVC techniques on each other by breaking into twos (dyads) and taking turns with each other. After several tries at this, hearing the results, both from partners with whom he had paired in dyads, and from when people spoke up about their improved results in front of the whole group, he finally relented, *"You know, you might be right about this. I can see how it is already working with the other women in this workshop, so I guess there's no harm in trying."*

If you want to practice with people who are dedicated to helping couples and organizations to create harmony and compassion in their lives, try doing a little "Googling" or surfing around the internet to find NVC, or "Compassionate Communication," support groups in your area.

Resistance Can Shift With Just One Person "getting off" of Their Position.

Sometimes the biggest changes can be experienced even if the other person would never agree to do the NVC process. One feisty young dude in my workshop in Australia argued that although he longed to have a resolution with his stubborn grandfather, he knew that his grandfather would never, ever budge from his righteous stance. I practically had to beg him to try the process with me playing the part of his grandfather, which he finally reluctantly agreed to do.

We found out by doing this process, that his grandfather longed to talk to him, but didn't know how to ask. About 5 minutes into this process, he realized that his grandfather loved him deeply, had never wanted to hurt him, and would have gone out of his way to help him, if he had just given his grandfather a chance.

I explained that the person who needed to change was not his grandfather, but himself. Because until he had forgiven his grandfather, and had given him permission to be just who he was, nothing was ever going to budge.

But now that he had opened a space within his own sub-conscious mind, his resistance had started to melt away. He now actually had the feeling that on some level he was reaching his grandfather without having to talk to him – and that from that moment on, a shift had happened between them. He had magically changed this long-time "resistant energetic" because the shift had happened first within him.

In a matter of a few minutes, he had opened up his heart and instantly transformed his life.

Over the next few days, find someone with whom you can practice NVC. If you anticipate any initial difficulty, it might be best to find someone who is **not** your partner. Get familiar with the format until you feel confident that you know how it works before you try it with you significant other.

Please be on the watch to eliminate feeling like you need to explain all the details, and get involved in a big "story." This will get you off-purpose. Have your practice-partner "call you" on this and vice-versa. Keep explanations and words to a bare minimum and just stick with the basic format.

By the way, you can have a same-sex practice-partner, where the friend helping you plays the opposite sex by role-playing as though they were your actual partner. Though, don't coach your practice-partner on how to respond – let them say what ever comes up for them.

You can start by using the basic format in the Process and Review section on page 72, which takes you through the steps and points out things to watch out for.

Will this process work if your Process-Partner has to play an antagonist's role?

The answer is "Yes!" You may have expectations of resistance from someone you believe is impossible to communicate with, and think "Why bother?" Allow your practice-partner to use their own intuition in coming up with the appropriate response for whatever question you direct to them. What they say may be completely different than what you would expect, and you might think, "They're doing it wrong. This person would *never* say *that!*"

Just give the process the 'benefit of the doubt' and continue until you yourself have a shift. It's not really about the other person anyway. It's about getting off of your predetermined stance and allowing something new to happen in your own thinking.

Air Your With-holds In a Safe Space – Time Out/ Withholds Sessions

Your Heart Wants to Be Heard – to Be Listened To Get It Out in the Open

One of the things most destructive to love and a successful relationship is feeling that you have to lie to your partner. Why would you have to lie? Perhaps you're doing something or have done something, you don't want your partner to know about. This sometimes happens when you are not able to communicate with your partner, and you've been withholding your resentment and anger for a very long time.

That's why I suggest setting up a format where it is safe to express things you have been withholding from your partner – a "withholds" session as it is commonly called. These sessions are effective when run at least once a week at a regular time; for example, Wednesday night at 8 pm until about 9 pm. Okay, there's a big game next Wednesday, so you switch it to Thursday or Tuesday, but way before Wednesday so it doesn't become an issue at the last minute.

Air Your Withholds In a Safe Space

First, you both agree when you go into this weekly meeting, that this is a time-out – a safe space, where you can talk about anything you want, knowing that this is not a time to argue, but to say how you feel, ask for what you want, and negotiate a positive outcome. It is meant to be a conciliatory, healing atmosphere, away from the heated anger of the moment when you first "withheld" your feelings or desire to express yourself. Now you can finally let go and stop withholding things you've wanted to say, but that you just couldn't bring yourself to expressing.

I don't know if you've heard of a talking stick – when you have a talking stick you talk until you're completely done and then you pass the stick to the next person. You can use the same technique without actually having to use a stick but you just *agree* before going into it, that *you* talk until you're done. So the partner might say, "Are you done now, sweetheart?" And you could say, "Well, there's one more thing that I want to say," and you say it.

Then your partner can say again, "Well, are you done now, honey?" and when you finally say, "Yes, I'm done," then you have "passed the stick" to the other person and now it is

their turn to speak.

The same thing can happen in relation to arguments, or settling a difference, or whatever it is that you want to talk about and you can be completely heard and listened to.

How a Couple in Australia Instantly Turned Around their Relationship

This attractive 40 something couple, Annie and Jerry, with 3 young children, ran a successful shop in a small town. Even though they worked together constantly, they hardly ever talked anymore. They both knew that the relationship was crumbling and, although they felt that workshops weren't private enough, they were willing to do a private session with me to see if they could mend what seemed to be impossibly broken.

The three of us sat on a big bed to talk about what was not working. Both of them were telling me what was wrong, but neither one was able to express it to each other.

I decided to try a withholds session with them, in which one person would speak as long as they wanted while they told the other person how they felt about what wasn't working for them. While she spoke, he was not allowed to interrupt. When she was done it would be his turn.

She said he never wanted to listen to her. If they ever were alone, he would get up and go outside and have a smoke so he wouldn't have to deal with her. This made her even more angry.

I reminded them to only speak from their feelings rather than make each other wrong. This was very hard for both of them because finger pointing was much easier and more comfortable. It created a cushion of separation between them so they wouldn't have to deal with their feelings.

None-the-less, several times one person or the other jumped-in angry, and blurted out that the other person was wrong. I kept stopping to remind them that they were not waiting for their turn, and that this is an essential part of the rules that make this process work so effectively. I reminded them that they needed to speak from their hearts about their feelings, rather than from an accusatory stance.

Gradually the whole tone changed when the truth of their feelings started coming out. She said she felt isolated and desperately unhappy because they couldn't talk to each other, and then she started sobbing uncontrollably.

He said he didn't realize that she felt this way. He didn't realize that his behavior was hurting her and he felt remorseful that he had hurt her.

After going through several rounds like this, they both started opening up more and more. Neither one of them had ever expressed what they were now saying in terms of their own feelings.

What an amazing difference this process made. Now for the first time in years they were actually speaking from their hearts about how they wanted so badly to make their marriage work and about the immense love they had for each other. They ended up both sobbing and hugging, resolving, with their renewed love, that they would keep communicating from their feelings and never let it go back to where it had gotten to before this evening had started.

Rules That Make the Withholds Session Work

Getting Started on Weekly Withholds Sessions

I suggest that you try a "Withhold Session" as soon as possible with your partner, before you forget that you want to try it. The idea is to set up one of these sessions the same day every week and the same time of day, so you always know what you are doing, say, on Wednesday between 5:30 and 6:30pm. Anything you have withheld for any reason that couldn't be expressed at the time you wanted to say it, goes on your "withholds list," that you bring with you to your weekly meeting.

At the end of this chapter you will find the format to use while you are practicing. The main idea is that one person talks (as long as they need to) while the other person silently listens. When the first person is done, the other person has their chance to be heard. This goes back and forth until everything on your withholds list has been aired. Always end these sessions with a melting hug (see pg 63).

How Withholding Feelings Can Result in an Unexpected Disaster

Let me give you an example: I had a woman attend an Intro I gave in Thailand, who was doing a "withholds" process with a random partner in the room. She started telling him everything she'd been withholding for *years*. It started out slowly, but she was building up to a faster and louder pace...

"I don't like the way you never listen to me; in fact you *never* hear what I want to say. You never let me tell you what I don't like, or what I am unhappy with. I am very angry with you. I wish we had never met. In fact, I've made a decision. I am giving you my notice now. I am leaving you!"

Fortunately, this was not her real partner. But this is what happens when people don't feel free to express themselves with each other. After 20 years, what seems like a perfectly wonderful marriage suddenly blows up. One partner or the other just announces one day, with no warning whatsoever, "I'm leaving you." And the other person never knew "what hit them!" This is much more common than you may think.

An Unexpected Announcement from a Husband

Here is an actual story of a woman I met whose husband was living in London with their two teen-aged sons and she was living in Thailand running a business. This exact thing happened to her. Even though they went months without seeing each other, she was shocked when her husband delivered the bad news.

They had lived apart for several years and only saw each other on Christmas and other holidays. They had arranged for their boys to visit or live in either location, depending on their educational needs. They mainly talked on the phone, but gradually, over time, even their phone conversations had become sparse. She never even noticed that something might be wrong because they were both running high-powered businesses that required most of their time.

This one year, they were making their plans for her to be in the U.K. for Christmas, and he told her, I have to see you right away. Can you come sooner? This was her first clue that something was wrong. When she got to London, he broke the shocking news that he that he wanted a temporary separation. When she got back to Thailand, things *really* started to unravel, and over the next few weeks, the 'separation' turned into him announcing, "I'm leaving you and I want a divorce." Apparently he was spending most of his free time with another woman and finally made the decision that he wanted to be with her instead of with his wife.

In retrospect, the sexual part of the relationship had never been very good. She was just not that interested in sex even though he was. She ignored his suggestions to improve their sex life. She was too busy raising the little boys. The whole sexual issue had just been swept under the carpet and was never fully addressed as it should have been.

With his bigger sexual appetite not being handled, it would have been obvious to anyone but her that he would have to have his needs met elsewhere, especially with her being out of the country for such extended periods. This is something that she was just not capable of handling and which she avoided to the point that she believed that it no longer existed. But it was there all along. If the two of them had been willing to address these problems when they were happening, it's entirely possible they could have worked something out and still be together today.

Hug Training

I bring up "hug training" at this point, because at the end of your withholds sessions, its always good to make a warm connection with a hug, just to confirm that you love each other and that you've peaceably resolved your issues.

A Conscious, Warm Body-to-Body Hug

A Body-to-Body hug is one great way to connect with your partner anytime you start feeling a little distant or need some non-verbal communication.

I got used to calling it a "proper" hug because when I was in the Screen Actor's class at Columbia Studios, my teacher told us we were going to learn how to do a "proper hug" on camera. The "wrong" way is what she called a "tent-stand." In a tent-stand, both people are hugging but without touching through the middle of their bodies – i.e., their butts are so far back that their combined stance looks like a tent > ⋀

The idea is for both people to push their butts in until both bodies are comfortably fitted together. Honest to Goddess, this is the way they do it for TV and movies. There is nothing sexual about it, just warm and friendly. People are overly careful about having their bodies touch anywhere near the middle because they don't want to create any sexual connotation or to be offensive. But it's still easy to comfortably hold each other through the mid-section of your bodies in a way in that your genitals are not jammed together.

I do this hug with anyone who is willing to try, women friends, men friends, relatives – everyone.

Now let's take this one step further and do a "melting hug."

Melting Hug

From the position I just described, you are breathing together in long, natural, rhythmic breaths so that you become attuned to the other person's vibration. You adjust your stance until it is totally comfortable for both people. You become very relaxed and just allow your bodies to melt into each other. Stay here for a few more breaths and then when it feels right, you come out of the hug. This might take as long as a minute or two.

Once you've tried it, you'll see that it wasn't so bad. I think you'll agree that it didn't feel sexual, only friendly. After awhile the melt-in should happen naturally. You can do this with anyone of any sex if they seem open to it.

Heart to Heart Hug

You can combine this with the melting hug above: With this hug, as the name implies, your hearts are touching. People tend to hug just the opposite way. So instead of fitting your head over your partner's right shoulder, you go for the left shoulder. The left side of your chests should touch each other's hearts so that your heart energies are combined in sweet synchronicity. This makes a hug even more emotionally close and loving.

Ian & Carmel's Naked Hug

We can't leave the subject of hugs without mentioning Ian & Carmel's Naked Hug to get a couple back on a loving vibration. In my travels I met Ian, a very interesting Brit. Ian told me he doesn't need my therapy. He and his wife, Carmel, solve all their problems with a naked hug.

He explains the way it works is if you are arguing and things are starting to escalate into a fight, one of them says, "Let's have a naked hug." The rule is that they both take their clothes off in any room *BUT* the bedroom and they *DO NOT* have sex afterwards. They have what is the equivalent of a melting hug, and stay in this position for up to 10 minutes, without talking, just waiting until all the anger has passed. Then they peacefully and calmly talk to each other about the "problem" without being angry. Ian said, "It's impossible to stay upset when you do this, and it instantly renews your love. Even works great when you aren't angry but just want to connect."

I have actually never tried this with a partner, but it sounds amazingly effective to me.

The one possible drawback is that the naked hug might be a "band-aid" approach, if what you are arguing about is not really the issue. Often people are angry about something much deeper that they've never resolved. The hurt still lurks in the background of everything they do. If you don't deal with it eventually, it will pop back up to bite you on the ass.

You just read a good example of this happening with my UK friend living in Thailand whose husband unexpectedly left her, so this is not something to take lightly.

Ousting Negatives to Clear Space for Positives

Which Does Your Heart Love, Positive Thoughts or Negative Thoughts?

When I first started learning about the metaphysical concepts that the Teutsches were teaching, I got this big

"Yes!" I *knew* that what they were saying was real. I could feel it in every bone in my body. This was all I could think about and I yearned to learn more. A more recent rendition of this concept is called the "Law of Attraction," and is being brilliantly presented by Abraham, brought through by Ester Hicks. You probably are familiar with the film, "The Secret" in which the law of attraction was the featured concept.

More likely than not, if you are reading this, you already understand the law of attraction and similar concepts. But if not, and you resonate with the following, you will never want to turn back.

First, what is metaphysics?

Metaphysical means beyond the physical, and refers to an idea, doctrine, or posited reality outside of human sensory  perception. In modern philosophical terminology, metaphysics refers to the studies of what cannot be reached through objective studies of material reality. As recently as thirty years ago, the whole idea of an extra-dimensional world was ridiculed by science, and was made to seem like utter nonsense, hocus-pocus, airy-fairy stuff.

A quote from 'Faith and Reason,' a one hour PBS documentary says this is changing: *"Recently, however, even as metaphysics has come under attack for its apparent lack of access to real knowledge, so has science begun to have its own difficulties in claiming absolute knowledge.*

Continual developments in our understanding of the human thought process reveals that science cannot solely be relied upon to explain reality, for the human mind cannot be seen as simply a mirror of the natural world. For example, since the act of scientific observation itself tends to produce the reality it hopes to explain, the so-called "truths" of science cannot be considered as final or objective.

This fact manifests itself over and over again, as scientific truths and laws continue to break down or yield to new and better explanations of reality. What becomes apparent, therefore, is that the process of human interpretation in the sciences, as elsewhere, is both variable and relative to the observer's viewpoint." [5]

The Advent of Quantum Physics

Now, with the advent of Quantum Physics, and it's being on the verge of acceptance by the scientific community, these notions are not so crazy after all.

What I've come to understand is, that the physical world is just a manifestation of our thoughts, or actually our "feelings," which are even more powerful than thoughts. This translates to the idea that the feelings and thoughts

---

5   A quote from 'Faith and Reason,' a one hour PBS documentary from The Educator's Guide, about the interaction between science and religion, both historically and today. It was developed by Simone Bloom Nathan, Media Education Consultants, and written by Margaret Wertheim.

that you project out into the Universe become what you attract.

Unlike negative thoughts and feelings adapted in your impressionable early childhood years unconsciously from your family, creating affirmations helps you change and attract what you want in the present moment.

Affirmations – Very Powerful if You Believe in Them

First, remember that our world, as we're experiencing it now, is a reflection or manifestation of our past. It doesn't represent who we are now – it is a reminder of who we used to be and the way we created it way back when. If we want things to change, we focus on sending out corrected thoughts, which bring us what we desire to experience in our new "present" as if it were already happening now. If we continuously dwell on what we don't like or what doesn't work, we will create more of the same. What we think about becomes what we get.

The trick is to suspend your old beliefs long enough to create new desirable patterns. Affirmations only work if they are believable enough that you can look your situation squarely in the face and say that it no longer exists. What exists now is your declaration or affirmation about the new way you picture it, as though it were happening now, regardless of the evidence to the contrary.

I started out with easy affirmations like, "I, Toni, now quickly and effortlessly find parking places right in front of the building where I am going." If I could really believe or "feel" that this is a true statement, then it would manifest as a reality in my physical world. It didn't take me long to become the "Queen of the Parking Spots."

That one was a slam-dunk, but manifesting a successful career, and money, took a lot longer, primarily, because I thought it would.

After years of practice working with these concepts, I am finally becoming a master of my own mind. A full training in mind-manifestation or the law of attraction is really too broad to address fully in this context, so if you can begin to comprehend it here, and take my word for it for the next few weeks, you will begin to see your positive affirmations manifest even before you've finished this book.

Without getting into all the technical details, let's just say that all of the above *is* true.

So if I could process out negative thoughts, then I could replace them with positive thoughts. True?

Yes and no. If I pick an affirmation that is out of my league (i.e., unbelievable), then I won't get results. My sub-conscious mind will be saying *"Hey, Toni, you're full of s...."* So a positive and a negative cancel each other out.

It takes understanding of your unconscious thoughts to create affirmations that work. In the review at the end of this section we are going to do a process on affirmations.

Generations Old Thought Patterns That Are Unconsciously Passed On

Often our thoughts are associated with generations-old patterns – those that have been passed to us by our parents, that came from our grand-parents, that came from our great grand-parents, and so on, back as far as seven generations, and perhaps even more. Recognizing that a thought or pattern isn't working for you gives you the opportunity to turn it around – to turn it into something positive.

In your marriage, when you can see you are not being yourself but being your mother, and the guy you married has changed into your dad, is this the point when you say, "I've had enough of this! The buck stops here!"

That point comes when you get tired enough of things not working, when you've been through several relationships that all *unbelievably* end up the same way – **then** you finally have the courage to say, "Alright, I'm ready to do whatever it takes to turn this around."

Remember, 90% of clearing a problem is recognizing that you *have* a problem. So knowing that you are living someone else's patterns, not necessarily what *you* would choose, means that you are 90% of the way to freedom from a particular pattern that you recognize you *don't* want.

So from now on, when you see yourself playing out a role of your mother or father's, stop right there and say, "This is **not** me. I choose to stop playing this role. I choose instead to (*fill in the blank*)."

The Victim Role

For example, let's say you recognize that you are playing a "victim" role.

There is one banana left in the kitchen. You were thinking of putting it in your smoothie. Your partner walks in and picks up the banana. You find yourself saying to your partner, "I was going to put that banana in my smoothie, but it's okay, you can have it," even though you really wanted it.

Coming from your "victim" stance, it's likely that your partner will give the banana back to you because you wanted to make him feel guilty – and it worked (victims and victimizers often reverse roles).

But what if you recognized your mistake and made this correction: "You know, that wasn't very truthful of me. I should have either said, 'That's my banana and it's going in my smoothie,' or to just decide that it *is* okay for him to have it, and not have said anything at all."

Then you've broken the pattern. Each time your "victim consciousness" comes up, you can recognize it and choose something else.

If your partner is a user or victimizer and you always play victim, then by *not* playing victim, it will help your partner to get off being a user too. Either he/she will start to change too, or may feel so uncomfortable when you step out of your traditional role, that they will be forced to adapt or leave.

Process Reviews and Exercises

PART 1

Relationship Covenant/Contract

If you've already jotted down some ideas in your notebook that you want to bring to your "Contract Negotiating Session," start expanding on them now and create a list.

For household chores, for example, make of list of everything that needs to be done. On a page using horizontal & vertical lines making little boxes about 1 ½ inches square, enter one of the items from the list into each box, cut the paper up into little squares and put them into a bowl in which the two of you can take turns drawing each item until they are all chosen. If you "draw" an item you don't want, you can negotiate a trade for something you both agree suits one or the other of you better, thus creating a contract that is fair and appropriate for your individual needs and talents – a win-win.

Maybe sometime this week, you can do a "mock negotiation" with a friend, (regardless of his/her sex), in which he or she can role-play the sex of your significant other.

If you are the listener playing the role of the other person's partner, and feel that this relationship contract would work for you (as the person you are – not what you *think* that person's partner would say, or that his/her partner would like to hear), then respond from your own personal truth. When it's your turn, you also will have the opportunity to try out *your* contract on neutral ears.

You will learn a lot from this process, and hopefully you can implement it with your partner (who will also pre-prepare *their* list) by setting up a meeting date.

You or your substitute partner might come to the conclusion, "You know, I thought I would be embarrassed to talk about such intimate stuff with someone like you, but it didn't matter in the least. In fact, it was energizing to realize that I can, and do, have very important things to say in creating a contract for my relationship, and I really appreciated your input."

PART 2
NVC–Compassionate Communication

NVC is something else you can practice with a friend (which I highly suggest you do before you practice it on your significant other). It takes some practice to use the NVC format without reverting back to old hostile patterns, and if you haven't practiced, you might have a partner who is reluctant to use NVC at all because it "doesn't work."

The following is the most basic format that you can practice with your partner, a friend, or a helpful person in your office:

1. When you......(don't pick up your socks)

2. I feel....(sad)

3. What I would prefer is....(that you pick them up and put them in the laundry hamper)

4. Would you be wiling to do this, at least for the time being?

5. Please repeat back to me what I have asked for so I know that you completely understand what I'm asking for and what you've agreed to.

If your partner leaves something out or twists the meaning into something other than what you meant, you point this out and ask them repeat the part(s) that were not quite right.

If your partner won't agree, at least you can "agree to disagree" and perhaps discuss it later when you've both had a chance to think about how you can both be satisfied with a modified resolution.

Things to watch out for:

Make sure you stick to feelings. If you were to say, "I feel that you are wrong," 'wrong' is not a feeling and it will only antagonize the other person.

Finger pointing and making someone wrong will produce the opposite effect you want. Being conciliatory, compassionate and forgiving is the stance that produces the best results.

If the first feeling you come up with isn't deep enough, I encourage digging up the "base" hurt or fear. "I feel disrespected. I feel angry. I feel hurt. I feel sad...." could be the progression, as one gets deeper and deeper into their feelings.

You might ask your friend to say how that process made them feel. Were there any "ah-ha" moments, any revelations or epiphanies on either side?

Remember to keep it simple: no explanations; no stories.

Please practice the NVC format at least once, and preferably 2 or 3 times this week.

There are lots of wonderful NVC therapists all over the country who give classes in NVC and support groups in almost every city as well.

PART 3
Withholds Session Format Practice

I suggest that you try a withholds session as soon as possible with your partner, before you forget that you wanted to try it.

Rules for the Withholds Session & Practice With a Partner

Here is the most important rule: Only one person can talk at a time. You or your partner can have as long as you want, uninterrupted.

The other person has to wait to comment, even if it takes 10 or 15 minutes.

The tendency to want to jump in and argue must be avoided at all costs, otherwise the meeting will not work. Chances are, by the time you (or your partner) get the opportunity to respond, you'll have forgotten what was so important at the moment you wanted to jump in and disagree.

When your partner has completely had his/her say, you ask, "Can I talk now?" Your partner may say, "No, I forgot one thing," or "No I'm not done yet." Then later, when he or she appears to be finished, you may ask again,

"Are you done yet?" If so, then *you* can start on your un-interrupted 10 or 15 minutes of talk time.

Try to stick to the Non-Violent Communication format when applicable. Also, be sure to give your partner a deep, melting hug at the end of your session.

Part 4

Affirmations

There's a process I learned in Sondra Ray's Loving Relationships Training, that I frequently use in my workshops. Whenever you come up with a negative thought about yourself, you write it down on the left side of a page with a vertical line down the middle. On the right side you change that thought into a positive affirmation. What is so brilliant about this model is that, when you notice that the affirmation seems "untrue" to you, you write *that* thought as another negative in the left, or negative column. Then you write another affirmation on the right, or positive column, and keep adjusting back and forth until you have an affirmation that you can live with.

So you can experience how really well this process works, please open your notebook and do the following:

Affirmation Process

Pick a clean page and draw a line vertically down the middle. Then draw a line across the top for the heading.

The left heading will say "Negative" and the right side will say "Positive."

[See an example of a similar affirmation-process "chart" on page 89]

Now write on the left side 5 things you don't like about yourself.

Perhaps you have written something like this on the left or Negative side:

"I don't like myself when I can't stand up to my partner and just say 'no' when that's what I really mean."

How could you change this statement into a positive that is believable?

In the right column, you might write:

"I can stand up to my partner and say NO."

Now, how does that make you feel? Are you comfortable saying this is true?

What is the underlying sub-conscious contradiction?

You're thinking, "It's not really true. I want to please her *so* much that my intentions just collapse when I'm around her, and I say "yes" to anything she wants."

So your affirmation really *doesn't* work for you.

If it doesn't seem real to you, your thought about that goes back on the left side:

"No, I can't really stand up to her."

What if you said, "I get the courage, more and more often, to stand up to my partner." Does this still sound like a lie?

You might think, "Well, this almost works for me – The more I realize that it hurts both of us for me not to be real, the more I can express my true feelings."

Hey, that's it! That's my affirmation!

So now you put this in the right column, "The more I realize that it hurts both of us for me not to be real, the more I can express my true feelings."

How about that for a positive affirmation? So you can see that what we are doing here is changing out all negatives into positives **that you can truly believe**.

If your "positive' sounds unrealistic, go back to the left Column and write the negative thought that comes up as a result. Then go to the next negative and work on that one in the same way.

Then process *that* one out. Keep going until you get an uncontested positive.

Then go to the next negative and work on that one in the same way.

You might work on 4 or 5 ideas today, but keep your notebook handy throughout the day so that if you have another negative thought about yourself, you can jot it down and work on it later when you have time.

You can also do this with a partner. It is the partner's job to do a reality check on their "positives" and make sure they will "stick."

When you are done, talk about how having done this makes you feel now.

I suggest that you take some time every day for the next week to write at least one affirmation, test its believability and process through it until you've created the perfect affirmation for yourself at this moment. As you get better and better at this, you eventually won't need to continue doing the testing process. In fact, even an affirmation from a few days before might need to be "upgraded" because you've already grown out of it.

Keep a list of positive affirmations and say them OUTLOUD every day as though you really believe them. Involving all the senses really works! Additionally, your affirmations will become *really* effective if you can visualize them being true in the present moment.

Secret 2:

Embracing Love by Starting
Within - with Yourself -
and Then Going for the
Highest Good for All

Chapter 4:

Our Own Sacred Heart – the Road to Self Love

Opening Your Perspective by Choosing the Road Less Travelled

W hen I was quite a bit younger, love was easy. I fell in love every day. But I didn't know anything about loving myself. In fact, self-love was kind of frowned on in my family and thought to be narcissistic.

On the other hand, it was considered *the* thing to do to be in service to everyone – everyone except yourself. We young ladies learned to give and give and give and never take anything for ourselves.

As it turned out, everything I learned was backwards, so it took me quite some to get my head screwed on right. I had to learn to love myself to bring up my level of self esteem enough to stop being a door mat and attracting men who treated me like one.

That's why, when I became familiar with the concept of going for the highest good for all concerned, although it made sense to me, it was still hard to figure out what the 'greatest good' actually was in any given situation, and still not let people walk all over me.

What a predicament! But after many years of practice I've finally found a happy balance between loving myself, considering how my actions effect other's lives around me, and negotiating win-win situations where I win, people in my sphere of influence win, and the planet wins.

Secret 2 gives you lots of ideas about how *you* too can find this balance. And now that you know about compassionate communication, you can use your feelings as a guide to create wins for you and your beloved.

Love – How Can I Count the Ways?

In this famous quote, "How do I love thee? Let me count the ways,"[6] from an Elizabeth Barrett Browning poem – instead of thinking of this as an ode to another person, you might think of it as a 'love proclamation' to yourself – or at least your higher self.

Looking outside your self for love is an illusion. I suggest that you might get used to thinking that "By loving myself first, I am better positioned to serve you," *you* being your beloved, or any one else in your life you think you need to love more than yourself.

In terms of Non-Violent Communication (NVC), or Compassionate Communication, you start with "you" –

---

6   The whole poem written by Elizabeth Barrett Browning (1806-1861) can be read by going to Appendix page 282.

your highest love. In spiritual terms "you" can be thought of as your higher self, the bigger more expansive part of you that encompasses your soul and "all that is" – Source, Goddess, or whatever you choose to call it. This love is the burning love and desire you have to merge with Source. On rare occasions when you stumble into merging with the Divine, this love is so great, that it takes your breath away as your heart expands into infinite ecstasy.

Loving yourself is popular among the "Cultural Creatives," and is one of the main spiritual concepts that slightly over one quarter of the adult population has embraced. The "Cultural Creatives" is a term penned by Paul H. Ray in his book, "The Cultural Creatives."[7] If you don't already know much about it, here is part of an interview by Peter Moore, Editor of Alternatives Magazine[8] (03/2001) giving a very brief overview on this subject:

"..."The Cultural Creatives" book, which has received a lot of attention since its publication (at the end of 2001), is the culmination of 14 years of sociological research about the emergence of a new culture, not just in America, but

---

7   Paul H. Ray, Ph.D. is executive vice president of American LIVES, Inc., a market research and opinion polling firm doing research on the lifestyles and values of Americans. He has published numerous articles on values and social change. He wrote and published The Cultural Creatives with his wife, Sherry Anderson, Ph.D. Their website is www.culturalcreatives.org.

8   Excerpted from an interview in online magazine, Alternatives: Resources for Cultural Creativity, entitled "The Cultural Creatives: We Are Everywhere – The 'InnerView' with Paul Ray" [You can read the rest of this interview by going to: http://www.alternativesmagazine.com/18/ray.html]

worldwide. It is an effort that combines the best of social sciences and hope for the future.

Peter Moore: *For the benefit of those who haven't read the book, how would you characterize "Cultural Creatives"?*

Paul Ray: *The Cultural Creatives are over 50 million Americans who care deeply about ecology and saving the planet, about relationships, peace and social justice, but also about authenticity, self-actualization, spirituality and self-expression. So surprisingly, they are both inner directed and socially concerned. In fact they're the activists, the contributors to good causes, much more than most other Americans.*

PM: *Why do you say "surprisingly"?*

PR: *There's a conventional media stereotype that anybody who is doing the work on their inner life is caught up in narcissism and ignoring the social problems of society. In fact, the data shows just exactly the opposite. The more people care about their inner life, the more they're concerned about the condition of the planet and human rights. There is a very strong positive correlation between doing the inner work and caring about ecological sustainability and social justice..."*

Love Starts Within and Radiates Outwards – Self Love Must Come First

Our inner work is to understand that love starts within, at the soul level. Our job is to learn to let our naturally loving 'beingness' radiate out into our surroundings, our family, our business, our world, our universe.

If you think that achieving this universally radiating love is beyond your reach, not to worry, it may not take as long as you think. After years practice, it has finally become part of who I am. The Universe arranged for me to become more humble to get me here. That's what I mean by going "kicking & screaming"...

You still might say, "Easier said than done."

If you grew up in a Catholic household like I did, you can probably imagine the kinds of self-esteem problems one might have developed. First, there's the whole idea of original sin, the concept that we come into this world as sinners. Ouch!

One predominant thought-form of this culture is "I'm not good enough." In Catholic Mass on Sunday we read from our 'missals,' "Lord, I am not worthy; through my fault, through my fault, through my most grievous fault..." It is no wonder that we feel guilty right off the bat before we've even *done* anything wrong.

What family in today's culture hasn't grown up with a big dose of "shame and blame," yet these are the two *most* negative emotions according to Dr. David Hawkins in his

"Scale of Consciousness," [9] from his thought provoking book, "Power vs. Force."

Guilt results from the feeling that one is responsible for harming others, either by omission or commission, leading to a feeling of responsibility and a desire to atone or repair, while shame is associated with the feeling of being negatively evaluated by others or by the self, resulting in feeling small, deficient, and worthless. Feeling powerless and passive could cause a tendency to disappear or escape from the situation.

So how do you get away from having negative feelings about yourself? It's not a good idea to push feelings and emotions away because they come back with a vengeance until you have been able to deal with them. You must first acknowledge that you are having these negative feelings, and then *know* that they are not you, but just baggage accumulated from generation upon generation of family patterns that have been passed down to you.

As I said before, "knowing" that you have a problem is 90% of its resolution. The other 10% is work on the subconscious part of your mind which Paul Ray calls the inner work. This entails the understanding that you don't have to own negative patterns you don't want.

---

9   Hawkins goes into great detail about the vibrational states of emotions. He describes which emotions have the highest vibrational states and which ones have the lowest. He explains many aspects of human experience through a *Scale of Consciousness*. Based on a logarithmic scale of 1 to 1000, all ideas, emotions, concepts, thoughts, works of art, literature and science, resonate at some level. Above the level of 200 these energies are considered nurturing, positive and "good" (Power). Below 200 are energies that are destructive, negative and "evil" (Force). Guilt and shame are the lowest vibrational emotions on the human scale.

For example, you might already be "in the mind of" someone who is self-deprecating, and as a result you might commiserate with others of like mind.

The aphorism that "Birds of a feather flock together," is another way to say this. But don't get too comfortable hanging out here. Wouldn't you rather "flock together" with people who consciously choose to love themselves and others?

Self Esteem – The Path to Giving & Receiving Love

You can think of "getting in the mind of" as becoming part of a larger group consciousness that you are hoping to incorporate as a good habit.

Example of How You Might Process-Out "Not Feeling Loved" [10]

Negative	Positive
I don't feel loved	I feel loved
Yeah, right	Sometimes I feel loved
Almost never	The more I love myself, the more I can love others.
I still don't feel loved	Every day, I look for ways that I can allow myself to feel more and more loved, both by others and myself.

Now, every time you have that negative thought about yourself you can use this or any other modified affirmation that works for you. Getting in "the mind of" feeling loved soon becomes a habit you can hang out with. Gradually you will start to attract more self-loving and compassionate people in your life. You will be putting out the right "vibe"

10 You might take a minute to review the Affirmation Process in the "Process Reviews and Exercises" section on Page 76

to attract love and the right people will unconsciously pick up on it.

Self-esteem issues can also be approached from the spiritual idea that we are all children of the Divine. I like to take that one step further and say that we *are* The Divine – co-creations between Goddess/God and our higher or soul-self. God's original thought is spun out into creating the matrix of actual physical manifestation of "itself," i.e., us as human beings. There is no time when we are *not* Divine beings, although we may have forgotten that we are. Let's get into the habit of thinking of ourselves as spiritual beings having an occasional human experience, not human beings having an occasional spiritual experience.

If you can comprehend all that, then it is just one easy step to seeing/feeling that you just cannot be *that* bad after all – "God loves me, I am a child of God, therefore I am entitled to feeling loved. I am love itself. I come from love. Love is my inheritance. I deserve love."

Daily work with affirmations eventually creates a bigger and bigger consciousness of things being right, in harmony, and of a divine order. The negative self-image, slowly but surely, starts to slip into the past.

Self-Love Mirror Exercise

Bill Cosby once told me about a little exercise you can do that really works to increase your self-esteem and is great for working on issues with your body: Stand naked in front of a full-length mirror. Then sing a sweet song to yourself about all the aspects of yourself that you love (or at least like). I cried the first time I tried this – I had never talked to my self in this way, much less sung myself a song. When you try this, really focus *only* on the positive things. You can do it over and over until you really *do* start to love and be more compassionate with yourself and your body. Your affirmation could be, "I love my self more and more, every day, in every way."

"The California Way to Natural Beauty"
Photo by Chris De Marco

What is Being Love?

"Being love" refers to who we actually are – goddesses & gods existing in a state of continuous, unending love. Without our bodies, love is all that is. Some people say God *is* love, and for me, that definition aptly describes the most pure, ecstatic state in which we can experience our 'beingness" – singly and collectively.

For many years I have been a meditator and this practice has brought me about as close to God as I can get without having sex. Believe it or not, even though you might not think of it this way, meditation can be extremely sensual, especially when consciously using some of the techniques for multiple orgasm described later in this book.

I could write a whole book just on meditation alone, but for now, I would like to suggest that one's *life* could become a meditation. This means opening your consciousness to include "all that is" – a state of just "being" in the moment, as much as you can. This does not mean pushing away your thoughts, but distancing yourself enough from them that they don't overcome you. If you pause every once in a while, and let your thoughts just float by like little clouds in your conscious vision, and then just "be" long enough to connect with your higher vision, this will get you out of being stuck in a difficult state of mind.

The *Instant Light Meditation* and How it Came to Be

In order to stay in touch with our higher selves and to access Divine intuition, I suggest frequent little meditations throughout the day. Because most of us just don't have time for extended meditation, little short ones of even a minute or two, bring us back in tune with 'being in the moment' where we can access the messages from our higher selves that we need for guidance.

My many years of long meditation practices have helped me to develop what I call "The Instant Light Meditation," which you can do frequently throughout your day, just to "take a breather," and clear your mind like a "reset" button for the brain. The more you do this, the easier it will be to connect with your mate in a loving state of mind.

Before we go to the meditation, I want you to know how it came about. "The Instant Light Meditation" evolved out of:

- 30 years of practicing meditation for an hour every day;

- Studying meditation over many years with some pretty impressive Gurus;

- 15 years of studying and practicing Tantra and learning to move Kundalini (Chi) energy around the body;

- Incorporating and using a yoga-like breath learned from 30 years of yoga practice.

The genesis of this practice began one day while I was doing my daily hour of meditation and I started having orgasms – just by breathing and moving energy, nothing else. This was so much fun that the next time I meditated I tried it again. And again, I would keep having orgasms for as long as I liked.

After a few weeks of this I decided to go back to my regular meditation practice because, after all, this was not really meditation. Or was it?

This process led to incorporating some of the elements that I experienced above into my general mediation practice. I've always felt that our entire lives can be a meditation – a living meditation, a conscious attunement with the Divine as we move through our every-day lives. My meditations started to become shorter and shorter and more and more frequent.

The Instant Light Meditation started to evolve a little at a time into what I do now to get instantly centered, and although it's not the least little bit sexual, it can be ecstatic as you imagine blissfully falling back into your larger, multi-dimensional self on the out-breath.

Doing this meditation, for even 30 seconds, gets you instantly centered:

The very act of breathing in and breathing out creates a flow of toroidal11 energy through and around the body, which can at the same time energize and center the mind-body-spirit continuum. Focusing on this flow opens me to the infinite Eternal nature of breath. When beginning The Instant Light Meditation you "say or think" the following mantras to the rhythm of a long, deep breath in and a long, slow, breath out (the in-breath and out-breath taking the same length of time):

Unio Mystica by A. Andrew Gonzalez
My impression of this beautiful art is that the
artist is a truly inspired mystic.

The Instant Light Meditation©

Mantra While Breathing In	Mantra While Breathing Out
Light	Bliss
Light	Bliss
Heavenly	Music
Heavenly	Music
Breath in	Breath out
Breath in	Breath out

When you are repeating the mantra on the first line, for example, as you breathe in you say and focus on "light." As you breathe out you say and focus on "bliss."

---

11 Described in more detail starting on page 141

You can do these in rounds, or hang out in any one of them for as long as it is effective. The idea is to quickly eliminate the need to "say or think" these mantras and just drift into the silence of your expanded consciousness.

Please use your own interpretation of what these "mantras" mean to you. With "Light – bliss," I imagine moving my breath and energy up my spine on the "in" breath, and, as the oxygen hits the center of the brain (the center of the third-eye chakra), I see an explosion of light or light energy, which some people refer to as "seeing the light."

On the "out" breath I imagine blissfully floating my energy back down through the body. Or, as I often meditate lying down, I've developed a technique where I feel like my head is falling backwards and my whole body follows, in a floating free fall that is absolute bliss once you get the hang of it.

For me, "Heavenly – music" is attuning to the sounds I hear inside my head. It reminds me of being in the country, lying in bed and listening to the music of crickets, near and far, joyfully harmonizing en-masse. Taken to the next level I sometimes imagine that I'm hearing and harmonizing with the sounds of the vibrational universe.

When thinking "Breath in – breath out," I focus on the body sensations of breathing – perhaps follow the breathing in and out, or just feeling the chest expanding and contracting.

You can do this meditation as often you want, for as little time as you want, throughout the day. Even one round of breathing can get me (or you) instantly centered. If it works for you, I hope you will continue using it forever.

I almost always start all of my longer meditations in the same way that I start "The Instant Light Meditation." For example, at the end of the day, when I lie down to go to sleep, I do the breathing with the mantras, and once I get to that centered place, I can stay there as long as I like, or as often happens, until I fall asleep.

Later on I will go into much more detail about how this process evolved through *The Five Techniques to Multiple Orgasm* and how you can use the same techniques for increasing the ecstasy you experience in your sexual practices.

After "Falling in Love" There Is "Being" Love

We've all done it at least once: We meet someone who makes us fall "head over heels" in love. We are infatuated, more about our own projections about the other person, than what is the actual truth. As it usually turns out, once we have spent a few months or a year with that other person, we start to see that they aren't who we thought they were. In fact, they may be nothing like our original perceptions, or what we had turned them into in our own minds.

This might be the time when a couple breaks up, especially if they don't have the tools to start effective communication. But, what happens if these now "lukewarm lovers" have already moved in together? Breaking up might be harder to do, and instead of communicating, depression sets in and they just stew in their own unhappiness. Perhaps the woman has become pregnant, they have already married and – then what? Are they to stay together forever just because it is the 'right thing to do' for the child?

Hopefully, your original perceptions about your lover had *some* element of truth, and you are willing to overlook the problems for long enough to work them out. This may be the time when you both decide to attend a relationships workshop to see it things can be saved.

If you were to get another chance, what would you do differently? As spiritual Goddess-God beings, our "default setting" is to automatically come from compassion and love. We embody love, and through meditation and understanding, will eventually come to feel that love radiating out from within ourselves to all that surrounds us – not just to our "love object" (the person we perceive we love) but to all human beings, seeing the beauty and love that they too embody. The Greeks called it agape, some call it Universal love, and others call it unconditional love.

If we are not getting in our own way, Divine intervention has us programmed to easily go towards that which works, to doing the best that we can do, to be loving beings, and to someday return to our blissful Source.

Being unconditionally loving doesn't mean that we have to invite a drunk on the street home to dinner, but that we can empathize with him, and acknowledge that he too embodies Divine essence. We can feel compassion and bless him. We don't have to like anyone, only to love them.

Now, what about our lover? Can we remain involved but unattached? We can show our love for our partner by letting them see who we truly are. In our more enlightened moments, possibly even while making love, we *become* these great beings of love and feel the love emanating back and forth between each other, and can merge into one great Goddess/God being of love. This is love at its best.

Tantric practices can bring us to this amazing state of unity faster than any other that I've studied. That is why there is quite a lot of emphasis on Tantric lovemaking, though in truth, Tantra is a lifestyle – a lifestyle in which one lives in the moment, comes from the heart, and feels connected to the very fabric of the Universe. Practicing Tantrikas know this, and have a great capacity for love. This is what is meant by "being" love.

If this sounds too scary to face, perhaps you can find an NVC (Non Violent Communication) support group and start practicing with other like-minded people who want to learn how to choose compassion over fear. As an alternative, you might consider a private phone consultation with myself, or someone who specializes in relationship counseling. Now you won't be alone in uncovering the beauty that we all are inside.

Process Reviews and Exercises

Part 1

Please take the time to do the "Self-Love Mirror Exercise" that I described on page 82. Once again: This really works to increase your self-esteem and is great for working on issues with your body: Stand naked in front of a full-length mirror. Then sing a sweet song to yourself about all the aspects of yourself that you love, or at least like.

You may find tears streaming down your face as you sing yourself this loving little song. When you try this, really focus *only* on the positive things. You can do it over and over until you really *do* start to love and be more compassionate with yourself and your body. Your affirmation could be, "I love my self more and more, every day, in every way."

Part 2

Ideas to Build "Being in the Mind Of" Loving Yourself

Here are some things to think about over the next week to increase your capacity for self-compassion and to be your own authentic self:

Explore for yourself what ultimate self-compassion looks like:

- Start looking for the stories you tell yourself that block your self-love. When you catch yourself doing this, just say "Delete. Erase. This is no longer who I am. I am a child of Goddess/God and I deserve to love myself. The truth is (fill in the blank)." Envision the thing you want to turn around with an affirmation in the present tense, as if it exists now, just as you want it. If you are having trouble with saying something exists now and your perception is that it doesn't, you can say something like, "I, (your name), now see that I am getting better and better every day, in every way." Another example: "I love my body more and more, every day."

- Choose self-acceptance and self-forgiveness over the negatives you continually repeat.

- Find out which parts of your own self-worth are non-negotiable, i.e., as a child of Goddess/God, this is who I am, and everything else is just a superstition.

- Explore ways to remember self-compassion even in challenging situations: For example, if someone puts you down, you immediately turn this around in your own mind and claim your own higher-self/ divine connection, acknowledging that Goddess/ God makes no mistakes and that you are perfect just as you are.

- To fine tune your affirmations you might want to refer to page 66 for the "Affirmation Process."

Chapter 5:
Setting Up a Sacred Relationship

Each of Our Sacred Hearts Are as Big as the Universe

Going for the Higher, Greatest Good

When there is a win-win attitude, a willingness to go for the greatest good, to express your own feelings with no need to put your beloved down, you can move to the next levels of sexual pleasure too. It is a lofty and welcome goal to reach such levels of ecstasy and bliss through loving your partner without being in competition.

Throughout this book we talk about going for the higher greatest good, and this actually translates to going for a higher spiritual understanding. We really don't want to be joined at the hip with our partner; we want to be strong in our own right, reaching for the heavens, for the highest good. So any marriage or union between a man and woman (including same sex couples) should include the concept that we are each powerful beings in ourselves, having self-esteem and self-love. Coming from here allows you to open you heart and receive love from the other person.

In the last section we were also talking about speaking from your feelings. When you learn to communicate your feelings, this opens you to discerning your partner's feelings too, thus becoming more compassionate.[12]

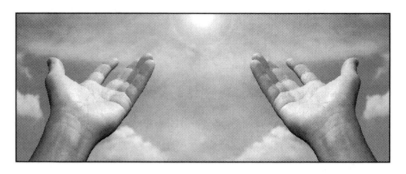

Radical Truth Telling

Perhaps the most important thing in maintaining a sacred relationship is promising to tell the truth. Without telling the truth, you cannot go to these higher levels of union. That said, it is quite an unusual relationship in which a couple is able to fully tell the truth, because that is just not the cultural norm.

Telling the truth does *not* mean dragging up all the dirt about the past, and telling every little thing that has happened to you. Though, it may be important to backtrack a little so your partner has more understanding, I am talking about going forward from now on.

You and your partner agree that you are going to be truthful. There is a compassionate way to do this, so you

---

12 If you haven't done so yet, go to page 49 to learn how to go more deeply into the actual practice of *Compassionate Communication*, which is also known as *Non-Violent Communication (NVC)*.

are not hurting the other person. Your goal to always tell compassionate truth can be learned through the practice of NVC.

In relationships these days, and for generations back, it has been considered okay for a man to have affairs while married. But, in today's society, it is not unusual for women to have affairs with other men.

There is no problem with this if it is agreed upon. However, if is *not* agreed upon by both partners, then you are back in the mode of not being truthful – or lying by withholding the truth – and that is very, very harmful to a relationship. A truly loving relationship cannot exist where truth is suppressed.

How can you love someone at the same time you are trying to hide the truth? It takes so much more energy to hide a lie than to tell the truth.

In Chapter 3 (Pg 43) we talked about relationship contracts, in which everything comes out into the open before you move in together. This is the way you want to set up your relationship if it is not going to be monogamous.

One of my partners expected me to be monogamous while he played around, and that didn't sit well with me. Perhaps if we had both agreed on extra-marital sex, i.e., an "open" relationship where we could have specific date nights with other people it may have worked out.

The point is that there are many different ways to work out unusual sexual configurations. The most important thing is that you agree on what works for you with your partner.

If you withhold the truth by not having an agreement with your partner and proceed as though nothing happened, this can destroy a relationship. Infidelity takes so much energy to hide, that it eventually kills the love, and the relationship.

Respecting Each Other's Wants and Needs

Another very important element is to respect each other's wants and needs. I can sometimes be a very needy person and can feel abandoned if my partner wants to do something by himself. But I have come to realize that if I want to have that same respect and ability myself, that I have to honor the other person's wants and needs, and the fact that they may want to do something different than what I want.

That might look like, I go to see one movie and you see the other one. We might take separate cars to the same party if we want to leave at different times. If he wants to go on a camping trip with the guys, then I'll figure out something to do with my girlfriends. There are always ways to work it out so we get our wants and needs met.

There is also the issue of maintaining our boundaries. That might look like I want to mediate every morning and not be disturbed, or I need to get my writing done everyday and not be interrupted. These considerations are natural and normal and need to be expressed and agreed upon, so there isn't any stickiness stepping into each other's lives in an inappropriate way.

Recognizing & Respecting Differences Between Male & Female Energies

If we understand the differences between male and female energy, then we are more likely to avoid power struggles. If the goal-oriented male/warrior is sensitive, open and has good self-esteem, he will welcome the soft and loving healing presence of a woman. Additionally, a man *can* find the feminine in himself, which helps him expand his capacity to understand women while still retaining his masculinity.

It is very important that men *and* women recognize they have within themselves, both a combination of masculine *and* feminine energy. Obviously a man is going to be more male than female. If he has a good balance of male and female energy emanating from his very 'beingness,' he can easily relate to a woman and experience the perks that come from knowing his own femaleness.

The same is true for women. By coming from the male part of their being, women can still be more feminine than masculine, but be able handle their own business, and do their own banking and other things that used to be relegated to the male.

The BIG Little-Known Secret to Making Love

Being in a loving relationship includes giving your partner what they need sexually too. It is *so* important to learn to touch your partner the way that he/she loves to be touched. That requires empathy, or *becoming* that other person to such an extent that it could be yourself that you are touching. When you are making love and merge with that person to such a great extent that *you can feel* what you are doing for them, then you've made it!

So, this is the secret to making love: Be *so* into pleasing your partner that it almost feels as if what you are doing to them, you are doing it to yourself. The thought you might express to yourself or to your partner could be, "Pleasuring you so pleases me, that I can feel *your* pleasure in my own body."

Spiritually speaking, it is true that we are doing that *all* the time anyway consciously or not. Any relationship, with any other person is just a relationship with ourselves – all is one, and one is all. The divine resides in all of us, and we are all part of the divine. The divine expresses itself individually through us but we are actually only one all-encompassing energy. If we can remember *that*, most of our problems would be resolved – between men and women, between families, and between countries.

When you can get to that place, the pleasure you receive in lovemaking will expand a million-fold. Not just a hundred or a thousand, but a million fold, and you will go to places you have never been. You will reach heights of pleasure and ecstasy you have never experienced. That's what unconditional love has to offer.

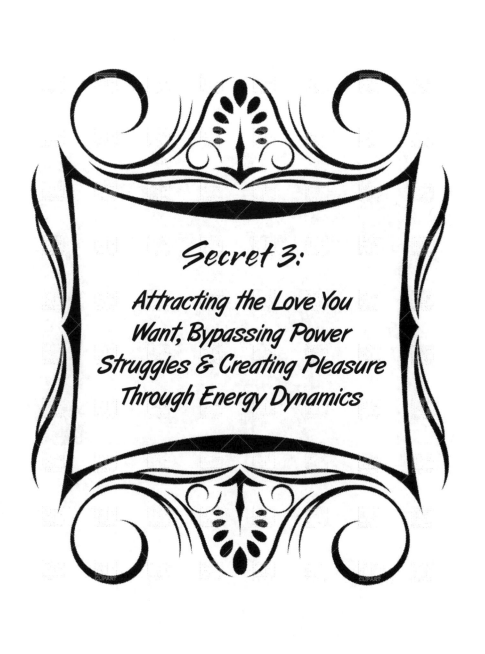

Secret 3:

Attracting the Love You Want, Bypassing Power Struggles & Creating Pleasure Through Energy Dynamics

Chapter 6:
Battle of the Sexes

Make Some Room for Your Heart — The Other Stuff Can Wait

Find the Love You Want & More Through Understanding Energy

Why was I going helter-skelter through my life, darting here and there to whatever grabbed my attention – was there something guiding me through a strange variety of seemingly unrelated experiences for which I myself, didn't even know the reason?

Why did it seem so important to me to learn about mind patterns that seem to control our destiny and at the same time be fascinated by the patterns an electron makes in a vacuum?

Why was I privileged to have a vision of the vibrating waveforms of our body's chakra system and later discover I was gifted to feel and see energy patterns of trees, plants and even rocks?

Why did I spend many hours in Author Janov's lab wearing electrodes, and watching a brain wave meter so I could discern the energy fluxuations that told me when I was in an Alpha, Beta, or Theta state?

Even though I wasn't at all interested in math or biology, why was I drawn to studying quantum physics and Einstein's theory of Relativity?

What in the world would attract me to a dowsing course? Why did I need to know "Touch for Health" and learn all the body's meridians and acupressure points? And finally, why was I so attracted to learning about Tantra when the only thing I knew about it was that it was about Sacred Sexuality?

Was I completely crazy?

Little did I know that during all those years of learning these different modalities, that they were training me about energy. It wasn't until I started writing this book that it started to dawn on me that all of these things *are* related because they led me to a deeper comprehension of the components or dynamics of energy.

All of this adds up to why I am now an authority on the dynamics of finding a perfect partner or learning how to reverse destructive relationship patterns through the Law of Attraction.

That we are living in a vibrational universe is a no-brainer for me, and fortunately for you, this knowledge can help you to transform your life.

When There's an Imbalance of Power, the Person Who Feels Oppressed Will Find Ways to Sabotage Their Partner

In my own life, because I learned all my patterns and habits from my mom and dad, they were both my best and my worst role models. As children, we grow up emulating our parents, close relatives or caretakers.

And where did my parents learn their thought patterns and habits? from their parents, of course. We inherit patterns from multiple generations of parents that are said to be traceable back seven generations. There's a biblical saying that "the sins of the fathers are visited upon the sons," implying that we pass on our negative habits and patterns from one generation to the next.

Conversely, The Great Law of the Iroquois suggests thinking seven generations ahead and basing the decisions and actions they make today on the propagation of benefits to their children seven generations into the future.

Abraham says "The only problem with leaving and going someplace else is that you take yourself with you. You take your vibrational habits and patterns with you."

In my parent's generation and culture, people were barely conscious of the harmful effects of the negative thinking that they were unconsciously passing on their children. I was raised in a very staunch Irish Catholic family and we really had to toe the line with my dad. My father was the "big bell" – the boss – and my mom, my four other sisters and myself, were subservient to my dad.

Since my dad did not feel very powerful in his life and in his career, he would assert his power with his family, especially with my mom and, because I was the oldest, with me. I was the kid that got the brunt of his power exertion, and it didn't feel very good to me. If I did not obey him, he would sometimes spank me or slap me. Mostly he would just get angry with me and yell a lot, or pretend he was going to hit me. In which case I would cringe to get ready for that blow – which psychologically, felt almost the same as actually getting swatted. So his behavior did not bode well with little Toni.

I was certainly not about to express myself, because it was either my Dad's way or the highway. There was nothing in between. I could never do anything right enough or good enough. Does this strike a chord somewhere inside you? If I came home with mostly A's and B's on my report card, he would ask why I got this C? For him, it was not about praise, or recognition, it was about one-ups-man-ship: "I am better than you and you have to do it my way."

Power Struggles – Getting Out of This Seemingly Endless Cycle/Circle

Example of Toni's Mom & Dad

He also lorded it over my mom, who had even less power than he did. During their nightly cocktail hour they would often get into these little spats. Maybe it wasn't even a spat, but he would say something and then she would shoot back a little dagger – by twisting his words to suit her repressed anger at him, as a way to get back at him for welding his power in a way that did not feel comfortable for her.

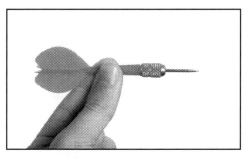

There was always a sub-current of hostility going on, and actually downright contempt for my dad, which is what happens in a relationship where people do not know how to express their feelings or can't say what they believe or think.

Growing up in this way does not provide the right role model that will help in attracting the right person in a relationship, like a husband or a partner.

How could things have gotten so bad between two people who love each other? My parent's generation wasn't comfortable about expressing their feelings because *their* parents weren't allowed to express themselves either. The release of anger, resentment, and contempt, instead of being straight-forward, would instead be expressed in the guise of innocence.

What happened to me as a result of this unseemly behavior between my parents? You guessed it – I would inevitably display the same behavior as my mom.

If my husband and I were at a cocktail party or giving a dinner party, this often became the background for providing a safe way for me to unload my feelings about my partner – in a seemingly innocuous way. Most people wouldn't even notice those little daggers of revenge, but when the friends weren't around, just like my dad and mom, we would get into a big fight over what I had said about him in front of them.

For me, all my men turned out to be like my dad. After my second marriage was over, I realized that I was continuously attracting relationships in which the man would eventually mirror my dad. Even if this new man was nothing like my dad, I would manage to turn him or the next guy into my dad every time.

This realization was so frightening to me that I finally stopped getting married. I didn't stop having relationships, but I became terrified of getting married. This seemed like the way to go because, after a while, I would subconsciously figure out a way to have the guy treat me like my dad, and that wasn't how I want to be treated.

My first mentor, Dr. Teutsch, helped me to realize that we seek out partners with patterns that perfectly mesh with our own. We attract each other with homing antennas or frequencies, which bring in partners whose family patterns perfectly mesh with the ones we learned at home.

It took me many years to get a more comprehensive understanding of why we do this. From a spiritual perspective, we are hoping to heal that primal relationship with one or both of our parents. We do this until we learn to love ourselves and form new patterns. Then our base vibration actually changes and we start attracting the partner more akin to what we have always wished for instead of what we always got.

Generations of Suppression

When people are victimized, they often become victimizers themselves. Unfortunately this vicious cycle has become most people's only role model in the home. This is a vicious cycle, because when people feel victimized and powerless (from a low sense self esteem), in order to build up their egos they usurp power and they bring others down in order to elevate themselves. This never works, because their perceived sense of power is false and unsatisfying.

They will never be able to drink the divine elixir of love and passion without first elevating their partners to equal standing and freeing each other from the tyranny of "bully-ism."

When a couple can be balanced through strong self-love and self-esteem, they are each strong and powerful in their own right: they don't need to compete and struggle to be on top. Both benefit by being side by side in a union that synergistically is even more powerful than either one of them by themselves.

Besides recognizing my own negative patterns, it took years and years to pare down enough of these negative patterns to be able to begin to attract better people in my life.

My Christmas Party Date

I once was on a first date with a guy I hardly knew and we were attending a Christmas party. Within a few minutes he started putting me down (he must have really liked me!). My "safety" antennas went up like a flag and I could actually "hear" what was *really* going on. In the past I would never have noticed it but I was getting better and better at seeing the "law of attraction" being played out in my life. My decision was "This man is not for me, get away from him as soon as possible." It was as though I had passed my Self-Esteem 101 class with an A+. Recognizing that my patterns were making another round, and that I didn't have to continue being a victim, was so much better for me in terms of emotional stability.

So now that I recognized that allowing myself to be put down was a family pattern/problem I had adapted, the solution was not far behind. I mentioned earlier that 90% of shifting a "problem" pattern is just the recognition that we have one. In other words, normally we keep doing the same things the same way because we have a blind spot about ourselves and we don't see our own patterns.

One clue that this is going on is that we tend to make judgments about other people and about things we don't like about ourselves. If we want to actually recognize our own patterns, start noticing what you can't stand about other people: They're just reflecting back to us, the negative signals we are putting out or once put out – the very areas we need to pay attention to in ourselves.

Finding Power and Using It with Gentle Strength, Love, and Compassion

By keeping communications open with your loved ones and others with whom you surround yourself, there is less chance of building up anger, contempt and resistance. Using your power to "lord it over" others will start to decrease as you learn to love yourself more. There will be less and less of a need to build yourself up by putting others down, the typical pattern of someone coming from low self-esteem.

The following are some positive things that you can focus on to develop the right use of power:

Go For a Win-Win Attitude for all People Involved

Being compassionate in the middle of an argument may be difficult at first, especially if things have elevated to a screaming-match, but it is doable. However, until you've become more facile with the win-win approach, it might even be necessary to remove yourself from the room until you have a chance to cool down enough to be rational.

First of all you start with the attitude that you will both win. It is not about one person losing and the other is going to win. When you argue, it's almost never about the issue at hand – it's just the same the old power struggle.

In a sacred relationship we agree to look at each other with the attitude that we are both going to go for the highest and greatest good for both of us so we can create a win-win. Now when I am arguing or trying not to argue, I remind myself to talk about my feelings.

Coming from talking about my feelings, I could say: I feel disappointed, I feel unloved, I feel rejected, I feel abandoned, or any other feeling I might be experiencing at the time.

For example, "I feel upset and sad when you talk to me that way. So what I prefer is that you figure out a way to talk to me without making me wrong."

This way I can begin to take part in working it out. "We have a problem that can be solved together. What I would prefer that you do is to look for a way that we can both be understood and create a win-win – for the benefit and the good everyone concerned."

Creating a Shift to Desires Driven by the Higher-Self, Not the Ego

When in a good marriage or a good relationship our desires are driven by our higher selves, accessed through our third eye and crown chakras, instead of being driven by our egos. There is nothing wrong with a good healthy ego because an ego is necessary to have strong self-esteem. We just need to learn to defer to our higher intuition without having our egos controlling our lives.

At times, individuals who are partners may want different things and there appears to be no resolution. We need to have an agreement that it is alright to disagree without trying to make each other wrong. In these situations we can make a decision to "agree to disagree," and have it be okay do things separately. There is no need to drag that person into our own stuff. It is okay to say what your preference is, and ask your partner to do what you prefer, but not have it be necessary for the other person to always agree.

Another thing that is important is negotiating for what you want. Allow yourself the willingness to be guided by your own intuition. Sometimes my intuition says, "Don't say that, it is the wrong thing to say at this time," and if I say it anyway I usually get into trouble.

Right use of Power – Finding the power within

Taking On a Willingness to be Guided By and to Follow Your Own Intuition

Your intuition can be a great guide and reference point to the options the Universe makes available, especially if you can get out of your own way and hear the message that is coming in. It takes a sense of humility to be able to let your intuition be your guide.

> *According to Jesus, the humble and least amongst us shall be elevated to the highest place – the first shall be last, and the last shall be first.*

Developing True Humility by Being in Tune with Your Own Divine Guidance

I used to think, "What's so great about being humble?" Whereas I always thought being humble was a negative, my opinion was based on the wrong ideas about what humility really means.

The dictionary describes humility as "*not proud or haughty: not arrogant or assertive; reflecting, expressing, or offered in a spirit of deference or submission.*"

From my own life experience I've developed a more spiritual interpretation of the above. I now perceive that humility equates with acknowledging and being in tune with my own power, tuning in to my Divine guidance, and allowing it to override my ego so that I can make correct decisions.

Now I am finally able to admit that I don't necessarily "know it all" as my ego would have me believe. So when I suggest developing true humility, it's about having a loving and confident kind of strength, bypassing thoughts having negative side effects in favor of those that tend to create a happy life.

Power Swinging Back to the Feminine

A few years ago I attended the California Governor's Conference on Women, where Deepak Chopra was speaking. He was talking about the correct use of power, especially as it concerns masculine energy in relation to feminine energy on the planet at this time. Paraphrasing what he said,

> *The pendulum has swung too far to the masculine side and when it reaches its apex it must swing back to the feminine. The world is in a state of crisis due to male dominance gone mad, and bringing us way too close to the brink of destruction.*

> *The loving feeling and nurturing of the feminine needs to come to the forefront before it is too late. This statement has only becomes more true as we approach the countdown to irreversible destruction of our planet's support systems – the ocean, the water, and the very air we breathe. Women have a very important message for the world in business, government and the environment.*

Another guest speaker at this event was the Dalai Lama himself, complete with a pair of rubber go-aheads and an orange cloth wrapped around his T-shirt. Now what could more humble than that? One has only to hear him speak for a short while to know that his masculine and feminine are well balanced. His most important message is to simply "be kind."

The Indian Nations Had a High Regard for Women's Wisdom

Within a tribe, when there was talk of war, the female elders were always consulted because women have high regard for humanity. They look for the most humane and fairest way to accomplish peace and/or wage war.

Attraction Is So Much More than Pheromones

I Can Attract Relationships Aligned with My Desires...
The idea of finding or being "The One"

Attracting the right person works if you're looking for a partner, even if you are already in a relationship. Once again, if your have been tuned into "The Secret," or perhaps Abraham-Hicks, according to the law of attraction you consciously or unconsciously, call into your field, people and circumstances that match your vibration. For example, if you think, feel, and believe that you can have what you want, you will probably get it.

Perhaps the thoughts you have every day about *not* being able to find the mate of your dreams, is the very thing that keeps you away from finding your soul mate. On the other hand, if you continue having thoughts that match your dreams, only then will someone in agreement with your desires manifest. Ester Hicks talks about launching continuous rockets of desire of what you prefer, and when you are in a vibrational match to the culmination of those desires, then you will attract the person who matches the intentions you've made along the way.

I remember talking to another of my mentors, Sondra Ray, who for years taught the "Loving Relationships Trainings", about the problems I was having with the man in my life. She said that my husband might have been my greatest teacher and therefore my greatest gift – he had taught me what I *didn't* want in a partner. What I didn't realize then was that I had launched so many of those "rockets of desire" along my trail, that what I *did* want was becoming increasingly clearer. I just didn't know where to go from there.

One thing I knew for sure – I didn't want to create the same results over and over again. And, I didn't want to get into any new relationships until I learned a lot more.

Learning to Love Myself

My real journey began with learning how to love myself. I didn't know it at the time, but when I left my parents behind, I still carried a low sense of self-esteem with me into all my new relationships. On the outside I was brave, brash, ready to take

on the world and make something of myself. On the inside I was a frightened little girl.

I encourage you to take a few moments to look inside at the child that still lives deep down inside you. For now, set aside some time and write down your ideas of what makes you who you are now. What would a healthy and conscious relationship mean for you? Who would you have to be to attract the person who makes you feel loved, honored, cherished, and adored?

That's where we're going with the understanding of how to have a conscious relationship. As you move along through this material, through getting to know yourself better, you will get a new perspective on who you really are. Once you understand yourself, you will have accumulated enough desires to bring your counterpart into your own life without even having to leave your own home. He/she will come knocking on your door.

No Need to Go Out – Your Perfect Mate Will Come Knocking on Your Door

This is a story about believing that I don't have to go looking for a man – that I could be home and a man would come knocking on my door.

It was the day before Christmas and I had no money for gifts for my two young children and I couldn't even buy a tree, but I was still determined to make this a great Christmas for my family.

It's now Christmas Eve, the kids are in bed, and there's a knock at my door. I open the door and lo and behold, standing in front of me is a tall handsome man with a big smile and a Christmas tree.

He explained that he'd had a crush on me from the moment we met (I had met him through a brief introduction by my ex-husband a few months before). He'd watched my coming and going from his apartment across the street and many times had wanted to talk to me but didn't. Now, he had gotten up the nerve to come and visit. On his way, he passed a place that was selling trees cheap (tomorrow was Christmas) and on impulse he bought one.

What an amazing Christmas present this turned out to be for me – especially because I was feeling so "down and out" and depressed. The tree – that was the cherry on the top of the Sundae! This was such a confirmation that I am being taken care of by my divine source.

We made love that night and the next day we celebrated Christmas with the kids. We all had great fun together. He stayed for a few weeks before he had to leave for California.

What other transformations happened in my life because of these results?

I have to admit that I was on the verge of trashing my carefully nurtured belief system of several-years, about the Universe providing everything I need, and despite the odds, that everything always turns out well.

What would have happened if I had not told myself "all is well"? And what if I *didn't* have the belief that I didn't have to go out looking for a man, that when the time was right that he would come knocking on my door?

I might have succumbed to a life of being unhappy and my children probably would have grown up unhappy too. I gave them the conditioning they needed to believe in themselves and to always remember, that no matter what, everything always works out even better than we think.

Chapter 7:

Empathic Sexual Energy - Initiating the Etheric Pleasure Centers

The Language of the Heart is Love & Compassion &
We Communicate Best Through the Loving Energy of Our Hearts

Energy – So Much More Than Meets the Eye

Etheric energy is not as mysterious as you might think. I had my first experience of "feeling" energy when someone suggested that I bring my palms close together to discover the sensation created between them. This simple approach to awakening sensitivity to energy really worked. It also worked with another person's hand facing my hand. You might first try this on yourself and then get someone else to do it with you. Almost everyone immediately feels the energy.

Here's how you do it: You spread out your hands so they're flat and bring your palms in towards each other (but not touching) until, when you get them 1 or 2 inches apart, you can start to feel, what I describe as a "cushy" kind of energy, as you pulse your hands in and out of the field between them (almost like your hands are bouncing off an invisible energy field).

Not long ago when I was in Australia, I took a 3-month, very thorough, energy healing course. Although I had studied many modalities of energy work in the past, this training served to bring it all together for me into one integrated whole.

We learned about measuring chakras, feeling their strengths and weaknesses, and gained through a mind-body-spirit approach, the ability to balance them. We also did a lot of training around being able to see colors, patterns, auras, and thought forms within a person's aura.

But it wasn't until a couple of years ago when I got back to the U.S. that I found out about Eric Pearl's, 'The Reconnection.' Very simply stated, this practice works by awakening to the energy between your hands in relation to the person who wants a healing. Okay, I was already familiar with the energy between my hands and intuiting different types of energy fields, so this seemed like a no-brainer.

It is actually such a simple approach, that anyone who can do the "moving palms close together" exercise, can do this too. That's why I'm recommending that by starting here, you can expand your sensations, both physical and extra-sensory, in perceiving how to "feel" energy. This will be handy to know for the *"Five Techniques for Multiple Orgasm."* So here's how it works:

You start by having your hands about a foot apart and varying the distance between them until you intuit a field with the same cushy, bouncy feeling you experienced above.

You could imagine going between gently squeezing a big invisible beach ball between your hands, and then as you slowly release, letting it push back your hands as the ball expands back out.

Once you can get a sense of the energy between your hands you can imagine that the bigger this ball grows, the bigger this feeling of energy grows between your hands. Eric suggests that this field of Source energy can be experienced as a force that gets stronger and bigger as your hands get wider and wider apart.

I won't go very deeply into the healing aspects here, but the healing happens between your hands, wherever your intuition guides you to place them. Having your hands between two places on or near a person's body, and without effort or having to do anything, except to get your expectations out of the way, the healing happens all by itself.

The whole point of going into all of this is to let you know that awakening to energy is something that you, too, can do. The whole of the following section deals with opening to energy, understanding it, and using it consciously to heal and enhance your life.

Physical Energy

Some of the types of physical energy that we've come to have some understanding about include: electricity, the force of magnetic attraction, heat energy, explosion, chemical bonding, smashing atoms, wind and physical phenomena created by forces of weather, movement of the planet, the phases of the moon causing energetic changes on planet Earth, etc., etc.

In addition to these, there are the more subtle energies which one normally doesn't see.

Empathic Sexual Energy: Initiating the Etheric Pleasure Centers

Presuming that you are now sharing honest communication with your partner, you can enter the next level of lovemaking:

By adding love to the "sex equation," you can relate to your partner through the heart, creating bonding and non-verbal communication, and often ecstasy beyond anything you may have experienced before.

We'll go into that in more depth in the next segment of this training, but to prepare you for that, we need to have a discussion about energy, quantum physics, chakras, and Einstein's Theory of Relativity. We'll find out how having an overview of these things can have a positive affect on your love-life.

Tuning Forks, Dowsing Tools, Pendulums

Dowsing with Harold McCoy

A few years ago, I had the pleasure of attending a workshop on dowsing with master dowser, Harold McCoy. Ever since then, using a dowsing tool has revolutionized the parts of my practice with clients who I'm teaching about the conscious movement of energy.

The Following is an Excerpt from an Article Written by a Student of dowser, Harold McCoy

"For several years, we have had a keen interest in the phenomenon of Dowsing and we have had the good fortune of learning from and working with Harold McCoy, an internationally recognized expert dowser and trustee of the American Society of Dowsers.

"At one point on an excursion to a cave with Herald she recalls, "The three of us were lined up on the path outside the cave, arms at our sides, staring straight ahead. Harold walked slowly towards us with his head down, pointing a sharp metal object directly at us. I was first.

"I stood there, completely still, watching the blunt instrument as it approached my solar plexus. Approximately five feet from my body, it began to turn, almost as if some invisible force was pushing it aside. "Boy, you have a lot of energy," Harold said, "Most people's energy field radiates out no more than a foot."

"Since childhood, I've always had a profound amount of energy, which has gotten me into trouble from time to time. I responded with, "So what else is new?" Everyone laughed. Harold continued to "check" my "aura" resonance. He walked toward me from the left, from behind, and on my right. The inverted L-shaped dowsing rod reacted in much the same way, turning five feet from me, no matter what direction.

"Yep, no doubt about it. You are one strong young lady," Harold said.

"I felt rather invincible as Harold moved on to Barbara. She stood quietly grinning as Harold measured her energy field. The rod turned one foot away from her on three sides, but when he measured Barbara on her left, the rod barely turned. "Oh, now that's interesting," Barbara exclaimed, "I fell off a ladder recently and my left shoulder has been giving me lots of trouble." None of us had been aware of this incident.

"Totally absorbed by the experiment, Sunny, the last to be "dowsed", was anxious not only to be tested, but to test as well. After her energy field checked out at a healthy two-foot circumference, Harold showed her how to hold the copper rod upright but tilted slightly downward in its loose brass casing so that it would take a definite force to move it left or right.

"Sunny was immediately successful as a neophyte dowser. She proceeded to dowse all of us, some nearby trees, even the dog. She has since decided to become an apprentice to Harold.

"Harold has recently founded the Ozark Research Institute, dedicated to investigating, researching and teaching the "power of thought." Dowsing or "water witching" an ancient method of locating underground water with the use of a wooden or metal hand-held instrument, is a common practice in many cultures as well as here in the Ozark bioregion. Any elder Ozarkian will have some sort of "witching" tale to tell.

"It has only been in the past decade, however, that dowsing has evolved into other realms. Not only are dowsers locating underground sources of water and minerals, they are becoming adept at locating lost objects and hidden treasures, many times from long distances by simply using a map of the given area along with a pointer and a pendulum."

Using a Dowsing Tool to Demonstrate How to Move Sexual Energy

I teach my clients how to consciously move their sexual energy by first showing them with a dowsing tool, how far their field extends. Then I can back up and ask them to move their field out to where I am standing, and the dowsing tool will instantly move to the side, as if the energy has made an invisible wall that pushes the tool to one side or the another, instead of continuing to point straight ahead.

It is my belief that mental, or thought energy, travels instantaneously through space and time. Therefore when I teach someone how to use a dowsing tool, it is their thought that in a nanosecond moves their energy to anyplace desired.

Using a Pendulum

The dowsing student went on to say, "The pendulum, a common tool used by most dowsers, is a small weighted object suspended from a cord or chain, held between the fingers. Allowed to swing freely, the pattern the pendulum makes swinging in a circular motion, clockwise or counterclockwise, forward or backwards, left or right – will determine the answer to any given question. The pendulum moves differently for each individual. For some, a "yes" will find the pendulum moving left and right, while for others it will move in a circular motion. Research with pendulum motion indicates that the movement can be attributed to subtle, involuntary autonomic muscle contractions of the wrist and arm in reaction to the subconscious."

When you're done with this section, perhaps you'll have a pretty clear idea of where all this is leading – right into the non-physical phenomena of spiritual or metaphysical energy.

Metaphysical Energy

The word, metaphysical, is derived from the Greek 'meta ta physika' (after the things of nature); referring to an idea, doctrine, or *posited reality outside of human sense perception*. It also means 'beyond the physical.'

The Energy-Matter Conundrum

Einstein's Theory of Relativity & Quantum Physics

Can you explain Einstein's Theory of Relativity? It all boils down to a realization that matter and energy are interchangeable. Energy equals matter. Physical stuff can be turned into energy. There are only points (matter) or waves (non-matter). All physical things in nature are expressed through waveforms and spirals. Black holes and white holes are compressed matter, and pure energy.

With infinitely small levels of energy (as in zero-point energy), does energy cease to be physical? Or does it just become increasingly harder to measure by human instrumentation? Is there really any difference between one type and the other? What was there before the Big Bang? Did some extraordinary force "conceive" or "think" the evolving physical universe into being? Are we just a thought that started in God's mind – first being energy and then becoming matter?

The "East Meets West" of Energy

Through our extra sensory perception (ESP) in our Third Eye chakra, we can often sense – feel, see and hear – these subtle energies, and we will be learning how to activate some of these through some simple techniques you can try including sensing energy between your palms.

The field of energy emanating from our bodies by a foot or two in all directions is simply called our "field." In this book we deal with the conscious movement of energy – mostly sexual energy initiated from the second, or sex, chakra. We are going to learn to send it around our body: up the spine, into the Third Eye chakra, and then send it down the front of the body, and back up to the base of the spine, where another cycle/circle continues. This is a process integral to understanding the *"Five Techniques for Multiple Orgasm."*

From quantum physics, we see that in the structure of an atom, that electrons and protons are relatively miles apart in vast amounts of space compared to the relatively tiny physical elements of the atom, and that even electrons can only be seen by the trails they leave. They are often observed as physical when being watched, but disappearing when not watched. Electrons can even divide into two and recombine as they are projected past a barrier in experimental lab conditions.

You might perceive an awesome kind of understanding starting to develop in your own mind. Maybe everything appearing physical is really metaphysical. Are thoughts like things? Do they become things? We don't have all the answers but these ideas might generate expansive concepts that could change the way we think about what is real and what isn't.

Demystifying Chakras

Most of the people reading this material have some kind of an idea about what Chakras are or have at least heard about them. If you don't know what they are, or if you are quite well versed in their qualities, the following will give you an idea of why I think they are important in the understanding of energy.

Many years ago I was sitting naked in front of a mirror in a lotus position and doing an open-eye meditation.

I started to notice a pattern of energy in the middle of my chest in alignment with my heart. At first I thought I was seeing the pulsation of my heartbeat and blood being pumped through my veins, creating energy patterns,

But it became more and more clear that what I was seeing was a coherent mandala-like circle of energy radiating out from the center. Then as this vision became more and more intense, I realized it had the shape of a donut (seen from above). Soon, I saw another similar, but smaller, whirling pattern around the belly button area.

And recently, after seeing the movie, *"Thrive,"* I now know that what I saw was the exact toroidal energy field that producer, Foster Gamble, had shown in a torus animation, but in side view. I had described this phenomenon as an invisible whirling vortex of energy spiraling out and rotating around a donut shape (which I learned in college, was a mathematical equation). I learned in this movie that they call this shape a torus.

Let's go back to a time *before* I had this vision: One day I'd wandered into a metaphysical bookstore and saw a drawing of an Eastern-Indian man, sitting in the lotus position, with a series of seven energy centers starting from the pelvic region, continuing up to the top of his head, painted with a progression of rainbow colors (from red to ultra-violet) depicting something called chakras. I didn't know what they were, or even how to pronounce the name, but I was certain that this was what I was seeing while I was having my vision.

Instead of each chakra being a different color, my chakras were light-derived, etheric, and combined pastel pinks, pale blues, pale greens, soft yellows and light violets – so very much like the torus animation I saw in *"Thrive."* [13] I was thrilled when I saw it in the movie – the energy, movement, and colors matched exactly what I had seen.

---

13 If you have access to the Internet, you might want to do a search for *"Thrive,"* the movie, and watch the trailer or the whole movie on YouTube.

Photo courtesy of www.thrivemovement.com

I felt so thankful, for seeing proof that what I saw was indeed real because, when I told my husband about seeing this vision of my chakras, he didn't even believe me. It was real to me and I've never forgotten this gift from the Universe, which eventually propelled me into searching for more information about the unseen world of energy. Even to this day, if I sit and meditate the same way I did then, I can see a hint of the same energy pulsations of my vision.

Since then, I have become a shamanic healer, and have studied a myriad of energetic healing modalities. I can feel energy with my hands, and if I close my eyes I can sometimes see energy patterns in people, plants, trees, and rocks. In my Tantric counseling practice, I train people in how to move energy, which helps lead them to understanding the spiritual-metaphysical aspects related to physical union with your beloved. Being able to move energy is a concept considered as "woo-woo" by Westerners but which is easily understood by Eastern cultures. Later in this book I will explain how similar techniques are the basis of Martial Arts.

But this is not the end of the story. "Thrive" taught me that toroidal energy patterns are so much more than just a pretty light show. The definition of a torus is a surface generated by a closed curve rotating about, but not intersecting or containing, an axis in its own plane.

However, Foster Gamble takes this further than just a mathematical definition, saying that toroidal energy is the basis of "free energy," and like free air, is everywhere. Unlike the so-called, perpetual motion machines of the past, energy devices of the future creating toroidal energy fields will make "energy access so inexpensive as to dramatically raise the quality of life for everyone." Terms like zero-point and cold fusion are now being referred to as the "New Energy" movement.

Photo courtesy of www.thrivemovement.com

He goes on to say, "A torus is not a closed or isolated system. It is open to the rest of the universe, as are galaxies, solar systems and the atoms that provide the electricity in our very own bodies. None of these are plugged into a wall socket. They all run off the infinite torque of the universe that is turning every system in existence."

Now, it makes total sense to me, that through the toroidal energy fields created by our chakras, the body has continuous access to the never-ending the energy of the Universe.

In view of the discussion above, the reality of Chakras, might seem more accessible, perhaps more physical, and at the same time energetic, possible and comprehensible in the light of understanding toroidal energy fields.

Einstein was one of the first to discover the magic of these fields, which eventually led to the development of Quantum Physics.

Waves and vibrations are an essential point in the understanding of energy, because that's what energy is. If energy and matter are interchangeable, most matter can be boiled-down to energy, waves, or vibrations.

The whirling vortexes of invisible energy of our chakra centers roughly correspond to our body's vital physical energy centers. Most experts agree that there are between 7 and 9 main Chakras, starting approximately the base of the spine (and/or related to the anus), and going all the way up to the top of the head (crown).

There are a few different "Chakra Systems" and descriptions, many of which are contradictory. From my extensive training in energy healing, here is my understanding of the progression of the Chakras and their related physical centers:

- Root/Base Chakra: Anus (family, money, home)

- Sex Chakra: Sexual Organs (Sex & sexual issues)

- Power Chakra: Belly Button and Spleen (power and survival issues)

- Solar Plexus Chakra: Solar Plexus, just below the heart (Self-esteem issues)

- Heart Chakra: Heart (Compassion and Love)

- Communication Chakra: Throat (Truth and Creativity)

- Third Eye (Ajna) Chakra: Forehead between the brows (Psychic abilities like ESP)

- Crown Chakra: Top of the head (connection between Heaven and Earth)

- [Soul-Star Chakra: Between 7 and 10 inches above the head (related to Higher Self)]

Progressing up the spine, each Chakra has increasingly finer and finer wave-lengths and amplitudes. Upon reaching the Crown Chakra a sound-wave of equal proportions would be high, fine, and perhaps not even be perceived by human ears.

When sexual energy is streamed up through each Chakra, the vibrations of each one are combined "additively" until they create octaves or melodic sounds like music – all in harmonious vibration with one another's wavelengths. Therefore, sexual energy is transformed from a single base vibration into a song of many harmonizing notes including fine, angelic highs. Experiencing ecstatic feelings in the body is our way of perceiving these energies.

It has been said that men and women differ because men come from the sex Chakra, and women come from the heart Chakra. Some people put down the grosser energy of the base and sex Chakras inferring that the higher, "finer" vibrations of the heart are more desirable. I disagree: Both energies are part of the whole and one is not better than the other. When combined you have music – therein lies the magic of God's creations.

Extra Sensory Perception

I think most people would agree that ESP, Extra Sensory Perception, involves perceiving beyond the five physical senses: Clairaudience, Clairvoyance, and Clairsentience. When a psychic is searching for intuitive visions, one mostly thinks of touching the forehead, the third eye center.*

*Note: If you have any stories about ESP, visions, intuitions, etheric voices, music from astral realms, or feelings of sensing spirits, please share them on our forum. [www.relatelovesex.com/forum]

An Accidental Meeting with a Psychic and My Dear Friend He Brought Through

Just before I started my worldwide journey, I wrote the script for a DVD I produced called *"Tantric Partner Yoga."* I brought in Robert Frey, a seasoned Tantra teacher, as my partner, and he did all the choreography for the DVD. During the editing process we had some long discussions about a series of DVDs I wanted to produce based on sacred sexuality. Unfortunately, just after the DVD editing was completed, Robert died due to a bizarre accident.

The draft I had written on this series ended up on the back burner while I went on the road for two years fulfilling my dream of transforming people's lives by teaching workshops in exotic, beautiful places all over the world. It was exhilarating to find people loving my trainings and actually having dramatic transformations as a result.

My Biggest Problem Was Not Being Famous Enough Yet

It was a huge boost to my confidence to land speaking gigs at two big holistic expos doing mini-trainings that I facilitated in both Sydney and Melbourne. Regardless of this success, everywhere else I went, it took a full month to build an email list, host "intros" and convince people that they should attend. The end result was once people got there, they loved it, but it was like pulling teeth to make workshops happen.

At one of those expos I stopped by a famous psychic's booth to ask if a friend I'd met in Thailand, had produced his television shows in Australia. But instead of answering my question, he said, *"Some one in your family named Robert wants to talk to you."* I had no recall of a family member named Robert but after trying to figure who Robert was, the psychic said, "Never mind, he just wants to tell you something," Robert is insisting, *"You must finish your DVD series. It will help you immeasurably and make you the success you deserve to be."* Of course the minute he said this, I knew it was Robert Frey.

Although this psychic was quite famous in Australia, I had never met or even heard of him before, and he had no way of knowing anything about me. No body else but Robert knew about those plans I had for the DVDs.

That brief encounter with Robert stoked up my determination to get my DVD project done as soon possible.

Now, over 3 years later, the DVD outline has turned into this book, and I'm planning to start the series of DVDs as soon as the book is published. Thanks to Robert and my accidental meeting with a psychic, my dreams are coming true.

There is no doubt in my mind that the veil between the physical and metaphysical is so thin that we can indeed intuit and perceive so much more than we are led believe through our cultural conditioning.

Just the simple and commonplace occurrence of thinking about someone, and having that friend call them, even from some place half-way across the planet, is a manifestation of energy being felt by another through thought-transmission, or extra-sensory-perception.

Kathleen Gildred's Story About Connecting with Her Mother

Here is a story told by my friend, Kathleen Gildred, about connecting with her mother long after she had died. It was excerpted from her mini-book "The Incredible 70's" and I pared it down a bit, leaving her writing intact:

"I'll never forget my friend Susie saying to me, the day after my mother drowned, 'You may not believe me, but I envy you - you had a relationship with your mother for 16 years I could never have with my mother, even if she lived to be 90!' This has stayed with me through the years. Even though she has not been with me, I've always felt her love, almost as tangible as if she were here.

Many years later, I was driving down the street, thinking about my mother and how much I loved her. Suddenly, I had an interesting thought: 'If I really believe what my metaphysical bookstore is all about, that means that my mother's soul is out there somewhere!' My more rational side asked my spiritual side, 'Do you really believe that?!' I had to think about it a moment, then, responded, 'Yes, I do!' then realized, 'Well then, with the love between us, I should be able to connect with her! Yes!' I thought, 'I do believe that!' So I put out to the Universe, 'Joyce Arlene Fischmann Gildred, wherever in the universe you are, I want to connect with you!' I said this over and over again, like a mantra, as if I was on short wave radio to the universe.

It was nighttime. I came home, and got in bed, lit a candle, meditated a few minutes, then blew the candle out and laid down. Suddenly, there was a flash of light in the room! My heart started beating really fast, and I had to calm myself down, reminding myself that I knew it was my mother, that I had called on her, that there was only love between us, and so there was nothing to be afraid of. This flash of light occurred again a couple weeks later, when my friend, Lance, and I were speaking about her, then again two weeks later. The third time, my mother and I communicated telepathically all night long.

As we communicated that night, at one point, I was telling her about the bookstore I was putting together, and that I had run out of available money I needed to complete it. She thought for a moment, then said, 'Don't worry about it, I'll take care of it.' I tried two more times to continue that conversation, with her finally saying, 'Really, it's handled! Next subject!' I had to pause to think of what else to talk about, since that subject was so up for me. The next day, my father called me, and said, "Honey, I just realized you have $10,000 in your mother's trust fund that you have coming to you (exactly the amount I needed). I'll write out a check for it and put it in the mail to you today'!

My mother and I communicated that entire night, and, as the sun came up in the morning, I realized it was October 2, which had been her birthday. I went outside, and had an amazing meditation, where, it was as if I went as far as I could go in my plane of consciousness (in an arch coming up from the earth to over my head), and she went as far as she could in hers (coming from the other side of me to the top of my head). When we connected, over my head, there was a mini-explosion of light, and then we were both going back and forth in an arc that was bright and angular, with pastel colors. I realized afterwards it was like a crystalline bridge between the planes that we had created through our love."

Psychically Connecting With Everyone We Know and Meet in Our Lives

I like Kathleen's story because it perfectly illustrates how a desire to connect with our loved ones, makes doing so absolutely possible. If we can communicate with our loved ones who have passed over, why not acknowledge the positive mental transmissions we could be making continuously with everyone we know and meet in our lives?

Why not? Because for some people it would be too scary to *even contemplate* that someone might be "picking up" on our thoughts. But what if mind reading is something we *already* do on an unconscious level?

From the point of view that through our Higher Selves we can *all* access Universal consciousness, we can and *do* access all that is, including thoughts, whether we do it unconsciously or not.

If you thought people could read your mind, would you change how you think? Fortunately, most people are not tuned-in enough to perceive someone else's thoughts. But people often say things in retrospect like, "I had a feeling that so-and-so was being underhanded with me."

When I talk about being "in the mind of..." something or someone, it means connecting on a spiritual, psychic or metaphysical level through the thoughts/vibrations we are projecting out into the Universe, whether consciously or unconsciously. I choose to do it consciously. I can, for example, choose to be in the mind of successful, happy people. As long as my thoughts stay centered there, then I am automatically connected with this "group mind" which elevates my consciousness.

Why is this important? Well, for one, we can *choose* to think harmonious thoughts so that we can link with other harmonious situations or people.

Also, we can start to program ourselves to give other people the "benefit of the doubt," i.e., to think of them in terms of getting better, being better, and imagining they *already are* who they want to be. They pick up on this at some level and it immediately elevates their consciousness about themselves and draws the two of you closer together.

Even *thinking* about condemning, judging, shaming, and blaming can hurt your friend in question because we all share the same Universal mind. Saying those things to others and gossiping about someone you know only magnifies a person's problems, therefore not helping them at all. Perhaps worst of all, you are hurting yourself too. The Universal law that what you put out, always comes back, makes *you* a victim of your own condemnation.

I still have 'a ways' to go with this myself (see pg. 34 about the Edwene Gaines' "21 Day Challenge"). Like Edwene, I made the commitment that for 21 days I would not gossip, criticize, complain (to others or even myself), or use any negative language. I made it all the way to day 19, but, because I slipped and gossiped about a friend, I had to start all over again. Having had to start over, actually, several times, it took me a couple of months to get through the challenge. I am grateful that because of this process, I've become super-conscious about where I direct my thoughts.

Conscious Energy Movement in Multiple Orgasms

Why have we spent so much time understanding energy and extra sensory perception? It leads us unto a deeper understanding of sexual energy and how it is so much more than just something purely physical – especially as is used in sacred sexual practice. For the ancient Indian Tantrikas, sex was just part of an overall lifestyle in which one experiences wholeness and oneness with all life – feeling as though they are an integral part of the very fabric of the Universe.

We cannot leave this discussion without going into one of the single most important things you will learn in this book, namely *The Five Techniques for Multiple Orgasm*. Why is this so important? Because once you are able to sustain extended sexual encounters, it is easier to arrive at the place where you merge in love, as "one-with-all-that-is," which in Hinduism and Buddhism is called Nirvana or enlightenment.

I am actually putting the cart ahead of the horse because a discussion of multiple orgasm requires some additional background information.

The background will be minimal for the time being, as you will grow into these techniques more and more each day, until finally, at the end of this book, you will not only have a full grasp of the concept, but you'll remember the techniques long *after* you've finished.

From Ancient India to the Modern Western World – A History of Sex and Spirit Through the Ages

Through the ages, cultural practices have evolved that helped bring people to their heart's desires. Enlightened beings have always known that integrating Divine energy – one's spiritual connection with body, mind, and emotion, creates a connected 'whole.' Whole-being consciousness is the most effective way to reach that which everyone hopes to achieve.

Detail of Vishnavath temple, Khajuraho, Madhya Pradesh, India

The Tantric Lifestyle of Ancient India

The Tantric lifestyle may have started thousands of years before the written word began to appear, but because there are no accurate records related to Tantra, we don't know much about the very early days of Tantra.

As many as 10,000 years ago, Eastern Indians worshiped the gods and goddesses, often through a deep connection with their sexuality, which they considered sacred. Tantra was a lifestyle, not a religion, that over millennia was adsorbed into the Indian culture in the form of many spiritual beliefs, practices, and eventually religions, such as Hinduism, Buddhism, Jainism and Sikhism.

Ancient Tantric spiritual practices and rituals are aimed to bring about an inner realization of the truth that, "Nothing exists that is not Divine."

Though the vast majority of scriptural Tantric teachings are not concerned with sexuality, in the popular imagination the term Tantra and the notion of superlative sex are indelibly linked. This probably arose from the fact that some of the more radical non-dual schools taught a form of sexual ritual as a way of entering into intensified and expanded states of awareness and dissolving mind-created boundaries.

We can see in ancient temple carvings that its presence was pervasive over all of India. There are only a few temples from early Tantric times that survived the barbarian invasions. Temple carvings from the Chandela temples of Khajuraho, deep in the jungles of central India, show how deeply sex was honored.

The temples were probably built between the tenth and fourteenth century AD. They are known for their depiction of erotic scenes and despite India being very conservative at this time, show an ancient history of the days when sex was celebrated in many different ways.

Everything from standard sex positions to what appear to be orgies can be found among stacks of statues on several of the Khajuraho temples.

Druids, Paganism, & Tantra: How Are They Alike?

Most people think that Tantra is just about sexual practices. However, Tantra was one of the world's oldest continually practiced Pagan traditions. Virtually all of the mystical concepts that come from India – Chakras, Kundalini, concepts of reincarnation, breath-work, yantra, mantras, etc. – were discovered and used by the Tantric peoples and absorbed into modern Vedic Hinduism.

In the ancient language of India, Sanskrit, dru means "tree" and vid means "knowledge." There is evidence that some ancient Tantricas moved West into Europe, bringing with them the knowledge of trees. The people with this knowledge were the dru-vids or druids.

Other sources, including Raphael Patai, author of "The Hebrew Goddess," show that the ancient Tantricas influenced the early Jews and Kabalists.

The Kama Sutra

Two thousand years before the present millennium, the evergreen classic, Kama Sutra, (a manual for married couples), was written in 35 a.d. by Vatsyayana (Vatsya). Kama Sutra literally means "the text devoted to pleasure."

According to one analyst, its focus, unlike Tantra, was not primarily spiritual, but physical.

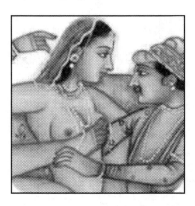

In Deepak Chopra's translation, "Kama Sutra & The Seven Spiritual Laws of Love," he says that the Kama Sutra can be read as "an antidote to shame."

What is Sexual Energy?

Our sexual energy is the driving force that makes us get up in the morning. It has been called Chi in the Far East and in India it is referred to as Kundalini. When this energy is engaged in a sensual experience, it is often perceived of as a pleasurable wave, like a shiver or vibration, flowing up through the body. In more sophisticated levels of Tantric practice, this flow can be like riding a river that goes on and on...

Practicing the ancient art of Tantra, a lifestyle in which love, connection to Spirit, and sacred sexuality all play an important role, has much to offer as a sensual guideline. Uniting a Tantric lifestyle with modern science and psychology, offers a path to having the best of the East and West – ancient wisdom grounded by today's practical teachings.

The study of Tantra is not just about sex; it is about feeling connected to the very fabric of the Universe – a loving connection to "all that is."

What is Tantric Energy?

Although Tantric energy needn't be sexual, in relation to a couples' sexual practices, the most basic description of Tantric energy, happens on an individual level in which, each sexual participant experiences a fusion of one's own Shiva, (male deity) and Shakti (female deity) energies.

Through the study of Martial Arts, many people have become familiar with the conscious movement of energy to accomplish physical feats, but most people don't know that this and other forms of moving energy can enhance your life as well as your sexuality – more on this to come.

The Eastern Concept of Energy Movement – the Basis of Multiple Orgasm

In learning multiple-orgasm, your focus will be on the natural movement of sexual energy up the spine, thus *not* having your genitals be your central point of interest.

As you imagine directing your sexual energy up your spine:

- you pause in the middle of the brain,

- turn the energy around and send it back down

- through the front of your body,

- sending it all the way down to the tips of your fingers and toes,

- and then back up to where you started at the last vertebrae of the spine, the coccyx.

Thus your energy is moving in a big oblong oval, circling around and around and around.

Moving your energy around your body in this fashion allows you to experience your whole body as an orgasmic instrument of pleasure. Your body becomes a fine instrument, analogous to a Stradivarius violin, with which you and your partner can learn to play each other exquisitely well.

This painting, *"Stradivarius Violin, God Of Wonders,"* by Andrzej Filipowicz, reminds me of how much I enjoy someone "playing" *my* body like a fine-tuned musical instrument.

The conscious movement of energy is an Eastern concept that we apply to modern sexual knowledge and techniques. You will learn more about "how" one moves energy in

Chapter 11. For now, let's just accept that it is as easy to do as it is to "intend" it. As a matter of fact, our thoughts or our intensions are indeed what move our entire universe.

Moving Kundalini Energy as a Sexual/Sensual Practice

When sexual energy is directed (or allowed) to flow up the spine, it is referred to, in the Indian vernacular, as the "rising of the Kundalini." It's often depicted as a waveform, much like a snake rising up your spine, in a wave-like fashion. Have you ever noticed the Western Medical Staff or insignia?[14] There are 2 snakes wrapped around a staff, which is a representation or an icon of ancient knowledge of our primal energy, our sexual energy, releasing up through the spine.

They are also called multiple orgasms because there can be many, many orgasms, streaming wave-like up your spine over a long period of time.

This is natural for a woman, but for a man, because ejaculations are accompanied by orgasms, men can be trained to experience the orgasms only (forestalling the ejaculatory

14 The Caduceus medical staff (with 2 snakes) also represents the spine [sushumna] while the serpents conduct spiritual currents [pranas] along the ida and pingala channels in a double helix pattern from the chakra at the base of the spine up to the pineal gland. Ref en.wikipedia.org/wiki/Caduceus

release), thus making multiple orgasms totally possible for a man as well.

Riding the Tantric Waves of Pleasure

At some of the highest points in lovemaking your pleasure expands way beyond the body, and at that point, I call it "Riding the Tantric waves of pleasure." It feels as if these sensual waves of pleasure are flowing right through you like a river, in wave after wave of ecstasy that actually shake and shiver the body to its very core.

When you first start practicing moving your sexual energy, you may have a series of little shivers, kriyas,[15] vibrating up your spine, which will seem insignificant in relation to the orgasms you are used to experiencing.

An orgasm is a pleasurable release. A small shiver is just the beginning of bigger ones. So *do* take notice. That is what you will want to look for when you first get started.

For the men who can't relate to having orgasms without ejaculating, think about the following.

Almost everyone has had a "piss shiver," which is what they call it in locker-room talk. This is what usually happens when you have to pee really badly: You have to hold it for a long time, and when you can finally get to somewhere where you can pee and finally release it, you experience a little shiver of pleasure that goes up your spine.

---

15 Kriya is a Sanskrit term that literally means "to move," which refers to various Yoga traditions in which the kundalini is in motion and shaking and quaking is occurring spontaneously.

That is actually a baby orgasm – a pleasurable release. Since the PC muscle group[16] is responsible for both urinary functions *and* penile strength related to orgasmic pleasure, it is no surprise that this should feel good. And by the way, it feels good to a woman too.

So, no man can tell me that he's never had an orgasm without ejaculating. It is this experience upon which you can build your new belief system about having orgasms being a separate function from having ejaculations.

So now men have a clue about "what to look for" in the way of nurturing even the smallest of orgasms, because they've experienced it before.

---

16 Toning the levator-ani group (of which the PC is the central muscle) will strengthen ejaculations and deepen the sensations of sexual arousal. Toning these muscles also brings fresh, oxygenated blood to the pelvis, which is essential for maintaining prostate health.

Contractions of the pelvic muscles are responsible for the ejaculatory process and essential for sexual pleasure. During sexual intercourse it is considered to be instrumental in increasing sensation, arousal, and strength of the orgasm in both men and women.

A healthy and strong PC muscle is associated with the control of normal urinary urges, while a weakened muscle is often considered to be a contributory factor in involuntary incontinence. Ref: Livestrong.com & http://en.wikipedia.org/wiki/Pubococcygeus_muscle

Martial Arts & Multiple Orgasms - Similar Techniques

Martial Arts Employ the Use of Directing Chi Energy — a Spiritual Concept

Believe me, the techniques for multiple orgasm are going to be about as sexy as a Karate chop. In fact the techniques are very much the same as used when executing a Karate chop. Remember, Martial Arts and Tantra both use techniques based on a spiritual concept – that of consciously moving invisible, spiritual energy through the body, to effect a desired result.

An introduction to "The Five Techniques for Multiple Orgasm" Through the Martial Arts

The First Technique: Breath

First there is the breath, in both Martial Arts and Tantra, the breath is your base. Long, slow, even, rhythmic breathing brings you to your center, gets you balanced, and allows you to maintain focus.

The Second Technique: The PC Pump

Then there is muscle control. In Tantra, we learn how to control the PC muscle (or pubococcygeus muscle). A strong PC is needed to deepen the sensations of sexual arousal and strength of the orgasm. Needless to say muscle control is extremely important in Karate too. In the five techniques, the PC is used to pump your sexual energy and oxygen up the spine and into the center of the brain where it can activate the release of "feel good" hormones. You will learn much more about this in Chapter 11, on page 207.

The Third Technique: Pelvic Movement

In a Karate chop, one imagines a line of power to direct one's chi beyond the extension of the arm (ideally to infinity) for the ultimate release of strength when executing the chop.

The body movement, which is next, in Karate would be akin to positioning your arm and hand for the chop, followed by the execution. In Tantra, as your passion builds, you are rotating your pelvis up and down for the "in and out" thrusting motion.

The Fourth Technique: Sound

And then there is the sound: Can you imagine a karate chop without that final yelp, **Yhow**!!!! – as the hand meets and shatters wood? No more than *I* can imagine repressing my body's natural urge to shout and proclaim my exploding pleasure as I'm having orgasms.

The Fifth Technique: Shiver & Shake It Till You Make It

Finally, there is the release of streams of orgasms which shakes and "shivers your timbers," as they ebb and flow, over and over again throughout your making love. We simulate orgasms by vibrating or shaking the body to stimulate the snake-like[17] waves of Kundalini energy flowing up the spine.

That can be likened to the pleasure received by an accomplished Marshall Arts practitioner, knowing that she has achieved this supernatural feat through her connection with Divine energy.

17 The Staff of Asclepius, the God of Medicine (with 1 snake). Greco-Roman god of medicine, son of Apollo (god of healing, truth, and prophecy) and the mortal princess, Coronis.

Process Reviews and Exercises

Energy Homework

If you haven't done so already, learn how to feel the energy between your palms as described earlier in this chapter.

Here's how you do it: You spread out your hands so they're flat and bring your palms in towards each other (but not touching) until, when you get them 1 or 2 inches apart, you can start to feel, what I describe as a "cushy" kind of energy, as you pulse your hands in and out of the field between them (almost like your hands are bouncing off an invisible energy field).

You might keep your notebooks open for now, and write down your ideas about Energy.

Write down some ideas about physical energy and it's myriad of forms.

What is energy? What are the different kinds of energy? How do we experience it? What's your perception of energy?

More than likely you already realize that most energy is something we can't see or touch.

Does this make it more real or less real? How do we know it's there? Which energy is "physical" and which is etheric or spiritual? Because scientists can't yet measure etheric energy, does that mean it doesn't exist?

If you are having trouble with any of this after writing down your thoughts about the above put your notes to the side and notice if anything changes later on.

What is Your Concept of Sexual Energy?

What is it? How can you use it? Feel free to grab your notebook and take a stab at describing it. It will just take a minute to jot down your thoughts about sexual energy.

Yes, You Are Right — It Is What You Say It Is — and More

Your sexual energy is the driving force of your life. In India it's called your Kundalini – sacred feminine energy or Shakti. It is an essential part of the life force in every living being. In China and Thailand it's called your Chi.

You unconsciously use your sexual energy to power your life (one of the primary ways it was intended to be used). Indeed, your sexual energy is your motivation for everything you do – for getting up in the morning, going to work, and for living your life with enthusiasm.

Without your Kundalini energy you would be like the walking dead. By the way, do you know anyone like that? Would you guess that they have been repressing their sexual energy for a very long time?

You can also *consciously* use this energy to stimulate yourself in many ways besides sexually, like for improving your memory, stimulating your genius, and birthing creative ideas to name a few.

In the context of this book, we are going to focus mostly on using sexual energy as a vehicle to having increased intimacy with your beloved, reaching ecstatic levels of pleasure, and eventually to experience enlightenment.

Secret 4:

Ramping Up Your Juiciness by Feeling the Difference Between Male & Female Energy

Chapter 8:
Loving Sensuality Enhances Sexuality

Guiding Your Partner Through the Language of the Heart – Love

If I Had Just Known Then What I Know Now...

It often seems baffling to me that so many married couples I've seen as clients, don't know one of the most basic things about the difference between male and female physiology – simply stated: Women take so much longer than men to be ready for sexual play.

And yet, that was our exact problem in my first marriage. It makes me realize that if simple facts like this could be taught in high-school or college, we wouldn't have such a high percentage of failed marriages.

Another thing that I wish I'd known when getting started out in my sex life, is how much easier and more intuitive sex would have been if I'd had kind of a "practice session" with my potential partners, in which we would take turns giving each other a sensual massage – and just stayed away from sex until we felt comfortable with knowing how our partner likes to be touched.

Whether you've just starting out dating someone or been married for years, you'll learn things in this section that will take the pressure off feeling like you have to perform. And you'll realize that you don't have to be a mind reader when it comes to knowing where to go with your husband or new lover.

Becoming One with Your Partner Is a Choice

It's an enlightened choice that you make to be of service to the other person. This doesn't mean giving yourself up or being too humble to enjoy your life. It just means you make choices from moment to moment if and how you want to be of service to that person.

In India it is considered one of the highest practices you can do for your beloved, to be of service to each other for each other's enlightenment. In a sacred relationship, obviously going for enlightenment would be one of the highest choices. Not everybody has that as a goal in their life, but certainly it is one of *my* goals. I don't feel we become enlightened but that we are already enlightened. We just have to remove the veil that hides us from our true, higher self.

Male & Female Energy — The Cultural & Physical Differences

I'd like to think that we were made to love each other. But what is it that makes us attractive to each other?

It is our differences that make our partners so attractive. "Feeling" into these differences is so important in understanding how sexual attractiveness works. I think people most would agree that opposites attract.

So whether you are in a heterosexual or a same-sex partnership, try sensing or feeling the differences between male-female energies. Feminine energy is receptive. Masculine energy extends outwards, or is giving.

As pointed out in Chapter 5 (page 103), even our bodies, whether male or female, have masculine and feminine sides: The whole right side of the body is masculine and the left side is feminine – except for the brain, which is totally the opposite.

It's quite common hear references to "right vs. left brain thinking." People are often said to be left or right brain dominant.

A person who is "left-brained" is said to be more logical, analytical and objective, while a person who is "right-brained" is said to be more intuitive, thoughtful and subjective. Ninety-five percent of right-handed people have left-hemisphere dominance for language.

Why are brain and body completely the opposite?...because the left side of our body is "wired" to the right side of our brain, and vice versa.

Although we don't know the reasoning of why nature created this crossover, it applies even to our eyes, which process a majority of their sensory data on opposite sides of the brain. Moreover, the right side of the brain controls muscles on the left side of the body, and the left side of the brain controls muscles on the right side of the body.

Our male-dominated culture, especially in education and science, discriminates against the right brain because it is a non-verbal or feminine form of intellect.

How does all of this apply to sexual relationship? Regardless of the kind of relationship you are in, sexual difference can create tremendous attraction and excitement.

One way to enhance this attraction includes doing opposite-sex role-playing during sex, which besides being a lot of fun, can help you to experience your partner in a completely different, and more understanding way.

Notice the tension between the two roles and the increase of excitement when the differences are exaggerated, including response to being submissive or dominant. Play with these feelings and allow them to bring you to places you've yet to visit.

The Physical Differences Between Men and Women

In this book, although we focus on enhancing the loving aspects of a relationship and finding the common ground, it's also important to note that men and women really *are* different physiologically and often psychologically as well.

A woman can come from her feminine juiciness, and a man can use his focused attention, to bring sex to whole new levels of ecstasy. Think of ways you can express your gender differences that make *you* feel sexy and attractive.

A man goes from 0 to 60 in about 10 seconds. A woman, well, she takes a *much* longer time according to Lori Grace Star, my first Tantra teacher. She is quoted saying that a man is like a pop-tart: you stick it in the toaster and in a couple of minutes it pops up and it's ready to go.

A woman is more like a casserole. You stick it in the oven and you wait, and you wait, and you wait, and you wait, and finally 45 minutes to an hour later you've got this bubbly, juicy, beautiful, casserole that's ready to go – and not only is it ready to go, it's ready to go for hours.

Once a woman gets juicy and has her first orgasm, she's ready to have a whole lot more orgasms and exponentially more fun, *and* she expects her partner to spend several more hours having fun with her.

So for men especially, it is important to learn the multiple orgasm techniques (also called full body orgasm techniques). Why? Because through these techniques men can learn to expand the period of time before they ejaculate, thus allowing women time to get as excited as men are from the beginning.

And there is one other very important reason: The longer a couple is engaged in multi-orgasmic (non-ejaculatory) sex, the better it gets. After several rounds of multiple-orgasms, you can tune into the rarified atmosphere of merging with the Divine, and what I call the "riding the Tantric wave of pleasure" (which we'll get into in more detail later).

The Dynamics of a Turn-On

The best way to turn up the excitement knob on a lukewarm relationship is to understand the dynamics of a 'turn-on.' When two people get together, once they get past the excitement of the first few sexual encounters, it starts to become apparent that that unless you can relate your wants, needs & preferences, and start to focus on how to please your partner, that sex can become very lack-luster. Added to that, if you are arguing and having communication problems, you're not likely to have sex at all.

The initial turn-on is easy. But how do you keep recreating excitement when the honeymoon is over? Here's where it's helpful to acknowledge, respect and work with the natural differences between men and women. Although there are certainly exceptions, it generally takes a woman longer to get turned on than a man.

Sensual Touching Tunes the Body Like a Fine Musical Instrument

Earlier, we learned about how circulating your sexual energy around your body allows you to experience your whole body as an orgasmic instrument of pleasure, which is why these techniques are often  referred to as full body orgasms. Your body becomes a fine-tuned instrument, analogous to a Stradivarius violin, with which you and your partner can learn to play each other exquisitely well. The key to making this work, is tuning in to higher frequency vibrations, which you will learn more thoroughly in Chapter 11.

Sex-Play Without Sex – Honing Your Sensual Appreciation

Especially in the beginning of a relationship you could use this approach: To build up to learning about your partner and what they like and don't like, it is fun and pleasurable to have a session that is devoted just to sensual touching, stroking, playing, and teasing, but no actual sex. This allows safety and non-commitment as options. It also hones your sensual appreciation, making you a better lover. Even if you've been with your beloved for a long time, if things have become somewhat lackluster, setting aside time just for sex play, can give your desire for romance an injection of renewal and excitement.

Sensual Massage Sessions Apart From Sex

When you are in a new relationship, another thing you can do to train your partner in how you like to be touched, is to both agree to give each other a one-hour sensual massage session. You do him. He does you. These sessions can be back to back or on different days. If you are planning a sumptuous evening home together without the kids, you might consider massaging each other the day before, or earlier in the same day. This should include enough time to sensually enhance your private lovemaking space, and have dinner preparations out of the way before you start.

A sensual massage doesn't necessarily have to be about sex. It could be about pleasuring that person just by stroking, teasing, and tantalizing.

Just like in lovemaking, you start out with long sensual strokes all over the back side of the body. Going from up the left leg, crossing over the back to the right shoulder and vice-versa on the other side integrates left and right brain and is very satisfying. This cross-over process is often referred to as activating your "cross-crawl" mechanism which causes stimulation to both sides of the brain.[18]

Then when every part has gotten attention, finish up the back side with massaging the buttocks and, a special treat, a perineum massage (see pg. 183).

Then you have your partner turn over, and after stroking the whole body start to focus on the inner thighs, once again crossing from one side of the body to the other, stroking over the breasts, and then back down to the opposite thigh. When stroking a woman it is very sensual for her to feel like you might touch her yoni[19] or vagina – glossing over it, stroking right along side of it – but never actually touching it – not until she is begging for it. During all of this be conscious of helping your partner to understand what you like and how you crave to be touched.

When she is finally begging for it you can build slowly and gradually into vaginal stroking, continuing the long strokes up the thighs and turn around at the breasts. Women so enjoy this kind of stroking you can do it for five minutes without changing. It also gives her a sense of security that

---

18 I learned this from Mary Press, a Santa Barbara chiropractor, who had us crawl around her office while waiting for our turn on her table. She told us that by crawling, babies develop nerve pathways, known as the "cross-crawl mechanism," which is used later to coordinate running, walking and dozens of other activities requiring left/right brain coordination. It is healthy for adults too.

19 Sanskrit meaning Entrance to the Garden or Sacred Temple.

you are not going to go further until she is ready. Once again, wait until she is begging before stroking her clitoris, and once asked, do this while continuing to stroke the inner thighs and breasts for a while more – this increases the anticipation of going further.

In this way build up with either partner, slowly and gently at first, building to more intensely sexual stroking, letting your partner guide you verbally or by showing placement of hands or fingers.

Guiding Your Partner in How You Like to Be Touched

Every time that partner does something that feels good you could say, "Mmmmmm that feels so good – I really love that, would you do it for a little longer?" Or if you are not liking what that partner is doing so much you could say something like "you know, that was really nice but it would be so much better if you could just do it a little bit harder," or a little bit softer, or whatever it is that you want 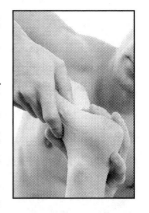 them to do. That way you're acknowledging what they've already done and asking them to make modifications that would work better for you.

By guiding your partner in this way, it doesn't take long for them to be trained as to how you like to be touched. Usually after a couple of sensual massage "coaching" sessions, they know what you like and want and are eager to please you. From then on you can relax more and just enjoy the stroking.

Your Partner's Loving Massage Is a Gift to Be Honored and Appreciated

Although giving your lover a sensual massage is not about tit for tat, you don't want them to go away feeling resentful because they are always willing to give you massages even though you might not have been reciprocating.

I learned this the hard way when my boyfriend of several years one day told me he had built up a lot of resentment about my never offering to give *him* a massage even though he often gave them to me. I thought he was a gift from God and that was just what he "does." I was always such a mess at the end of the day – often with so much physical discomfort or pain that I was just incapable of giving *anyone* a massage. None-the-less, there were times when I could have offered him a massage, but didn't even think of it. I felt really remorseful when I realized how self-centered I had been.

So don't think of it in terms of tit for tat, think of it in terms of being of service to the other person. "What can I do to enhance my partner's sense of happiness and feelings of self-esteem and love?" It never hurts to ask your lover what you can do for them.

Since a man can also learn to relax through a short sensual massage, this might be a way to your man's heart even when he thinks he is too tired to make love. Men like sensual teasing too, so if you want to take this further, you might try giving him a little stimulation where it really matters.

Men Have it Better When They Pleasure Their Lover First

If you are a man, and things have gotten off to an auspicious start, you might think you want your partner to jump right into something like playing with your member, but please wait. It's always a good idea to pleasure the woman first, mainly because if you get too excited you might go over the top, and then it's pretty much all over before your mate has even had a chance to get really warmed up.

Awaken a Woman's Desire Through Sensual Massage

There is no place on the body that isn't an erogenous zone in a woman, and it should be that way in a man too. Once you learn to wake up your body, every single way that somebody can touch you feels sensual and possibly sexual. So keep that in mind, that any place you touch on the body is an erogenous zone. Later I will expand on the *Tantric Wave of Pleasure* that we can tune into like the frequency on a radio dial, which brings our total body into ecstatic pleasure with every part becoming an erogenous zone.

The Three T's of Sensually Stroking a Woman

Often all that a woman wants is just to be cuddled or touched or held. Doing this might lead to an invitation to some conscious stroking.

There is nothing more wonderful for a woman than just to be stroked. In the process of being stroked, a skillful partner can use the Three T's – *tease, tantalize* and *titillate* – to enhance his beloved's excitement and anticipation.

In the process of a sensual massage you build up very slowly to get into the areas of genital touching. Once she has been stroked for awhile, you can start using the 3 T's: techniques to tease, tantalize and titillate, like gingerly stroking around the vulva (vaginal lips) and lightly stroking the breasts and nipples. Nipple stimulation provides a direct connection to her clitoris without even touching her there. In this way you can have her actually begging you to go into touching the more sensual areas of her body.

You want to wake up her desires in a non-confrontational and safe way. You should always ask permission to go into direct sexual touching. If a woman trusts you and you have not scared her by going too quickly, you can awaken her desires in ways that feel safe and natural. Please, never proceed to the next level until you are absolutely certain that your partner's ready. If you are not sure, ask. She should be begging you to take the next step if she is truly ready.

In terms of getting a woman excited enough for inner vaginal play and possibly penetration, it can take about 10 to 20 minutes of stroking and teasing foreplay. Later we'll get into where to go with a woman from here, but for now let it suffice to say that foreplay leads to exciting the clitoris, finding and holding the goddess-spot (G-spot), and getting a woman up to speed through simultaneous stroking of the clitoris and G-spot. In Chapter 12, we go into much more detail about G-spot stimulation for both sexes.

How a Woman Can Please a Man Through Sensual Massage

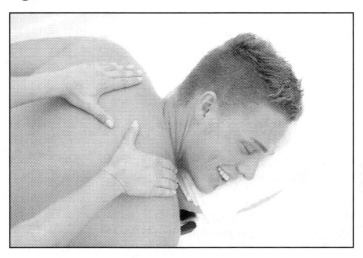

Sensual Massage for a Man

Men also enjoy the inner-thigh stroking, so when you have finished sensually stroking his back, turn him over to his front side. You can stroke his whole body by crossing sides like you've done on the back, and as you stroke by his lingam (penis, Sanskrit for *Wand of Fire*), you can either tease him a bit by ignoring it, or just almost accidently touching it as you pass by. A few more strokes like this and you might ask him if he would like his lingam stroked. This signals him that it is a good idea to get permission for sexual touching from both partners. Always ask first.

Another Thing a Man Loves – a Perineum Massage

The perineum is the area of skin directly underneath a man's genital region.[20]

---

20 By the way, women have a perineum too, roughly between the vagina and the rectum, and can benefit from a perineum massage while pregnant to avoid tearing of this area during childbirth.

About the size of a quarter, the perineum is just on the other side of the prostate, which can be massaged from the outside. Later you will find out how to massage the prostate from the inside as well. The job of the prostate is to provide an excretion that helps to give sperm mobility, and a prolonged life – so massage from either side, is beneficial for the prostate.

Relaxation is important in setting the stage for pleasure. It helps a man to relax by putting him into a warm bath followed by a sensual massage.

You can start by massaging his back to get him relaxed, followed by a brief massage on the arms and legs, and feet Then slowly work up the legs to the behind. A "butt massage" feels so good to a man, that if you go from here to his inner thighs, he will open his legs wider to accommodate your working massage lubricant into the perineum area, which he is sure to love.

Using your index and middle fingertips, you can touch, rub, stroke or press his perineum, trying various sensations and pressures including deep vibration. Using your other hand, you can continue stroking his behind for additional arousal. You might ask him, "Do you like this? Do you want it any deeper, stronger, or faster?

Now that you've touched on your man's sensitive nerve, try to locate the round bulb of tissue of his prostate. Continue massaging here in the same way, also communicating to make sure he is still liking your strokes.

Receiving perineum and or prostate stimulation may cause feelings of having to go to the bathroom. Usually this feeling goes away once he gets more relaxed. Later on, when describing the inner prostate massage, you will see that prostate stimulation can cause a release of throbbing or pulsing spasms, a vibrational response that I describe as multi-orgasmic sensations. If your man does find pleasure from this experience, it might set him over the top if you rhythmically or irregularly press on his prostate gland. It is even possible for men to orgasm through prostate stimulation alone. Clean fingers with clipped, smoothly filed nails are safe for male perineum and prostate stimulation.

Tantric Partner Yoga

Not a strict or rigorous practice, partner yoga involves some basic yoga poses with each other in which you can relax and get more intimate. I offer this in my DVD, *"Tantric Partner Yoga,"* [21] in which you are guided through an hour of floor exercises. Once you learn the poses, there is a pared-down 15-minute option, and a series of Tantric of sex poses. Although during the partner yoga there is no sexual touching, it could be a prelude to such possibilities as having dinner together, going to bed, watching a movie, or *maybe* having sex. The important thing is that you are massaging, touching, relaxing, relating, and stretching, indirectly creating the biggest benefit of all – you will be improving and enhancing your intimacy!

---

21 Found at www.tantrapartneryoga.com

Secret 5:

Trusting Your Passion as You
Learn Orgasmic Response and
Build Your Ecstatic Energy

Chapter 9:

Foreplay and Setting the Space for Lovemaking

Now that you know how to ask lovingly, do you know what to ask for

Shock and Awe and a New Life Ahead

As I was leaving my first Tantric workshop I was praying I wouldn't be struck by lightening and disappear in a puff of smoke. Not that I really thought that would happen, but all my old Catholic stuff came up when I started reviewing what I'd been through in the last three days. I'd long since had a mutual parting from the Church for choosing a life deemed sinful by them, but joyful and natural to me.

None-the-less, I certainly wasn't the same person who arrived at this training that I was when I left. At least, all that had been buried in my past had risen to the surface and I'd had a chance to reassess where I stood now.

I was pleased to see how much I had grown in so short a time. I no longer felt shy about many of the "private" things I'd participated in during this workshop, and I'd had plenty of opportunities to abandon all my old worn-out mores. I actually loved this new feeling of freedom – it felt like a breath of fresh air.

One of those things was watching my seminar leader, the amazing and outrageous Lori Grace Star, clad only in a bikini, lie down on the floor in front of 30 couples and after a few minutes of doing some specific breathing and motions, and without touching herself, started having a series of multiple orgasms. "Wow!," I thought, "I'll have whatever she had! How'd she do that?"

Unless you were raised on a different planet, it's my guess that regardless of your gender, you may experience many similar feelings in going through this next section, which you might call shock and awe. It will feel awesome to be given the amount of control and flexibility you'll develop in regards to what new possibilities lie ahead in your immeasurably enhanced sensual life and relationship. Just jump on in and enjoy!

Foreplay Doesn't Have to Start in Bed – It Could Happen All Day Long

This is one of the *good* things that I learned from my mom and dad. He would often come into the kitchen while my mom was cooking, quietly tip-toe up behind my mother, and he'd kiss her on the back of the neck, saying, "I love you."

Those little things are really appreciated by a woman. It doesn't have to happen in the kitchen. It can happen anywhere – An intimate dinner before lovemaking can do wonders for foreplay, and it sets the tone for intimacy before you even get into the bedroom.

There is just nothing more wonderful than to be acknowledged by your partner by showing them your love. During the day, touch them a little bit – connect with them physically. It doesn't have to be distracting – just give them enough attention to make them feel that they are appreciated and loved.

If your partner is working and doesn't like being disturbed, you still might be able to get away with this if you make it clear that it is not your intention to bother them, but just to provide a moment of loving acknowledgement.

Day-time Melting Hug

Another nice thing to do during the day is to give your partner a really great melting 'heart to heart' hug (see pg.64). This way the left sides of your chests are touching each others' hearts so that your heart energies are lovingly combined.

You can also do this before you start having sex, or you can do it during sex. Of course, during sex you are probably doing this horizontally, but there is nothing more wonderful than a delicious relaxing cuddle at some point during lovemaking. Or if the two of you get out of sync

 with each other and one of you has to slow down, this would also be a great time to have a cuddly hug.

If you want to connect with your partner and *not* have sex with them at that moment, a melting hug also works wonders just to perk things up.

Creating the Time & Space for Lovemaking

One of *the most important tips* that "HE♥RTGASM!" offers is to set up a regular time for making love on a weekly basis. Planning ahead avoids getting into one of those situations where you're working or taking care of the kids from breakfast to bed, and never taking the time to have sex. That's the worst! It's the quickest way to lose the sexual connection with your partner and that feeling of being loving. Mark this special night in your calendar every week and be rigorous in keeping this sacred date.

Sensual Enhancement of Your Space

Now let's talk about decorating or enhancing your love-making space:

I think you'll agree that the essentials for making your space a sensual experience would be enhancing anything visual, or related to smell, touch, taste, and hearing. All of these enhancements can be achieved through soft, sensual lighting; melodic, sexy music; candles, incense, essential oils; sensuous clothing; erotic elixirs and aphrodisiacs – aphrodisiacs, well, that's a whole book in itself! Actually you might want to check out Linda De Villers' "*Simple, Sexy Food*," claimed to be an aphrodisiac cookbook like no other.

Another thing you and your beloved can do before making love is to go out for dinner at some sexy place, and order food that is completely intoxicating and sensual. And of course if you are in the mood, you can also arrange to do that at home.

A Surprise Treat for Your Lover

In my workshops, people love learning more about sensual experiencing. So at the apex of the 3-day training, we throw a Puja, a kind of a sensual party, where one of the processes is to pick a partner and take turns in giving them a delicious sensual taste – something like a strawberry dipped in chocolate while they are blindfolded.

And, of course, your mate would love to experience something like this at home too. You can surprise your beloved by announcing that you need to blindfold them so that you can give them a special treat. This could kick off a wonderful evening at home with just the two of you.

The Sensual Massage Leading to Lovemaking

Besides setting intentions, which you'll learn about next, *before* you jump into making love try starting with a short sensual massage. The 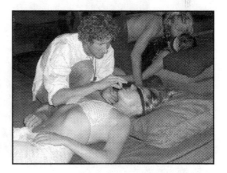 massage can be less than five minutes each – enough time to allow both partners to relax and not feel that there's any need to proceed to the next step until they are really feeling open and receptive.

Chapter 10:
Coaching Your Partner Until You Get What You Want

The Ultimate Coach Is Your Own Heart

Setting Intentions Before Making Love

When a couple comes together with the intention of making love, you might be sitting facing each other on your bed. I always like to start with the Namaste greeting, *"The Divine in me recognizes and honors the Divine in you."* Once you have agreed that you are both Divine, you step out of the box you normally live in, and open to the world of Source energy itself.

The next most important thing is to take a few minutes to connect by stating your intentions for each other. During this connection, take this opportunity to look lovingly into your partner's eyes, and say what your intentions are both for yourself, and for what you'd like to do in the way of giving your partner pleasure. Then your partner will do the same. It could go something like this:

"I am so excited about sharing this loving space with you tonight, darling. I have such great intentions to give you as much pleasure as you are willing to receive. That would be one of *my* greatest pleasures.

Another thing I would like to experience tonight is for you to stimulate my clitoris and goddess spot at the same time to see if I can have female ejaculation, Amrita.[22] That would be absolutely fabulous for me! Now, what would *your* intentions be for tonight?"

Then her partner could talk specifically about what he would like to receive and his intentions for her too.

This sets the whole tone for what's possible for the two of you, and sets you on a path of experiencing exactly what you are in the mood for.

This might segue into sitting in a Yab-Yum position in which you and your partner are sitting almost belly to belly (his legs are crossed, she is sitting on his lap with her legs wrapped around his waist). This brings you very close together, and if desired, with your genitals touching. Once situated you can do the "Hands on Heart" process, and then snuggle into kissing, hugging, and whatever happens naturally.

---

22 Amrita or Amrit, Nectar of the Goddess, or Golden Nectar, is the female ejaculatory fluid from a vaginal orgasm referred to in ancient scriptures as the drink of the gods granting them immortality.

The Huge Benefits of Pleasuring the Woman First

It does make more sense in terms of the overall way to enhance and arouse each other, for the man to pleasure the woman first. Since men tend to get excited very quickly, and women start more slowly, she can be helped to get "up to his speed" by a considerate lover. She needs to reach a place where she is way more open, more excited and more responsive than where she started before she is really ready to please him.

When she gets up to speed, *then* a man can start asking her for what would please *him* and for what makes *him* feel good. The man gets huge benefits from doing this because, once her passions are aroused, it's hard to stop her. Women are wild, sexual creatures who are much more passionate than men. They feel exponentially more pleasure than men, and can go forever once they get started. More importantly, a woman can bring a man to ecstatic feelings and erotic places which he may never have experienced, once he gets her going first. At that point a man's pleasure can be enhanced and prolonged indefinitely and exponentially, especially if you are both doing the techniques for multiple orgasm.

Once You Are Making Love

You don't have to start in any particular place. Once you've set your intentions, it's best to have no goals. Having goal-oriented sex is kind of a throwback to the dinosaur age because now with the secrets of Tantric love-making, you learn to always be going at the same pace your partner is going. If you are consciously breathing together its easy to stay in sync. Even if you are *not* consciously breathing together, it becomes as natural as "walking in step," in which you become entrained to each other's gait, and in this case, to each other's breathing. If one partner is getting ahead or behind the other, you could always tell that partner, "Lets stop for a minute and have a cuddle" – i.e., a sweet, luxurious hug – to sort of reset the clock and get started all over again.

Ask Your Partner for What You Want and Actually Get It!

Break the Spell of Vocal Withholding

First of all, we need to break the spell of vocal withholding. A lot of people think you can break the mood by talking when you are having sex. But there's no rule that you can't coach your partner while you're having sex. Now that you've set your intentions and told your partner what you want, you can perfect and fine-tune your coaching when he's giving you what you've asked for. If you say it in the right way – a loving and compassionate way that continues to enhance the mood you're in, it's totally acceptable and actually good to be able to tell your partner what's working and not working for you.

An example of this is when you might not be appreciating the unconscious way your partner is stroking you. Chances are he/she has drifted off somewhere else, or is thinking about what they are going to do, rather than being in the present moment.

No One Is a Mind Reader

Because no one is a mind reader, the best time to tell your partner about something that's not working (even though it may break the mood a bit), is to say something when you have a chance, rather than to let it go on and on. If your partner thinks he/she is doing something you like and certainly isn't aware that the stroke he/she is doing is irritating, then a kind reminder will bring him/her back to the moment.

So what you might say is, *"Darling, I really love the way you are stroking me, but if you do it for too long it starts to become irritating. What would work better is for you to vary the stroking so that it is soft sometimes and harder at other times, and a little more conscious, frankly, 'cause we would connect better if you were to think about how I am feeling as you are stroking me."*

I frequently find that 'irritation' happens when your partner has a certain goal in mind and is trying to reach that goal. The best thing for him/her to do is just drop the agenda and really focus on the moment. In fact, my advice for anyone in this situation is to become more conscious. Feel how you are feeling, feel yourself touching your partner – let yourself experience them through how they are touching you – you can get right into their body and feel what their body feels.

If you are applying all of the suggestions in this section, you should be all ready to proceed in your ecstatic lovemaking with no problems. Practice makes perfect.

Getting It Right In Retrospect: Taking Time Out for Your Sexual Withholds

Let's go back to a time *before* you're having sex, where you and your partner could maybe have a little "time out," or "withholds" session, where you just sit and talk and listen to each other, and explain a particular facet of how you like to have sex. This probably wouldn't include the actual "demonstration by touching" part, which you would be doing during a sensual massage.

However this is an opportunity to go back and forth with each other, a process which we call a "withholds" session (Pg. 59). This doesn't necessarily mean you're withholding things, but that you could actually be talking about something that you're willing to release that you didn't feel was appropriate at the time it happened.

Here's How a Sexual Withhold Looks When Aired in a Withholds Session

For instance, the woman might tell her partner how she prefers it to be. She might start by saying something like, "You know, it was wonderful making love to you last night, but there were a couple of things that I thought I might talk about today because I didn't want to break the mood that we were in. I feel that you got started with me in genital touching a little bit before I was ready for it, and if I'd been a little more in tune with myself, it probably would have been appropriate to say something right on the spot. But I was sort of caught up in the moment, and I thought it would have been better to go ahead than to stop and have a break. But generally speaking, I think that it would be good if we could spend a little more time in the foreplay part of sex than we've been spending lately."

Now the other person can respond, or say whatever it is that they want to say, whether it relates to what you've just said or not. So it might go something like, "You know I *did* get the sense that you weren't quite with me last night and it probably *would* have been better if we had sort of slowed down, and if we had changed something about the way it was going, but I *did* get very excited, and I was just anxious to get on with it. I wasn't listening to my *own* intuition – so I appreciate that feedback and I'll be more aware of it in the future."

He might continue by saying "Now there is one more thing since we're talking about last night that *I* would like to say. What I would appreciate is if you would spend longer with me in the genital touching: I feel you don't realize how important that is to me, and that the more continuous it is, the better. So would you be willing to let me coach you in those circumstances, so you can learn how and when I like to be touched that way?"

She might say, "Oh that's a *great* idea. Sometimes I just don't feel confident when I touch you and I *would* love to learn to do that better."

So that's just a brief example of how you can use a short meeting during the next day where you set aside some time to discuss things that are difficult to say in the heat of making love.

Squelching Fear of Expressing Sexually & Asking for What You Want

A lot of people are afraid to talk about sex, and certainly about asking for how they like to be touched, or how they like to touch their partners. The following is a process that you can do with your beloved, or with a friend of either sex, to turn your fears into deeper modes of satisfaction by becoming a "sexual communicator."

Sometimes it helps to do this with a stranger, not actually touching each other, so you get used to expressing things that you feel are intimate and considered "inexpressible" around other people. This will also get you used to hearing somebody reply to you with words you are not used to hearing and getting a greater depth of understanding about your partner through what someone else thinks. This gets you "un-shy" really quickly.

By the way, in my workshops and/or if you are doing this with a friend, it is only talk. You would never be actually touching – only expressing the way you like it. Realizing that there's nothing at risk by just using words, eventually your partner will start to feel comfortable in both of these circumstances.

The rule of thumb is, praise what they are doing and then ask for a change. This is something I learned from Margot Anand, a brilliant Tantra teacher who has facilitated over 2000 workshops worldwide that focus on Tantric sex. There is just nothing better than to be able to tell somebody what you want, in a loving and praising way, and actually being able to get it.

Process Reviews and Exercises

Do the following process at least once this week:

My Sexual Preferences: The "What I Like in Sex" Process

Three Different Stages

In this process we go through all three different stages in order to get used to expressing and voicing what we want in a loving and compassionate way with our real or our surrogate partner.

'Compassion' is the keyword, so that the other person doesn't feel 'less than' or 'not good enough,' and all the things that come up (based on their childhood experiences) that are normal for people. We always want to make our partner feel safe and loved.

You start talking about how you like to be aroused, and of course this is different for every person. At the halfway mark of each stage, the partner who did not start speaking, now takes his/her turn to expresses how they like to be touched at that particular stage.

Then you take turns talking about getting into the sexual excitement stage and how you like sensual touching to be done. Then, finally, you segue into talking about how you both like to be touched in the passionate and highly aroused stage.

The Arousal Stage

Sitting facing each other, one partner just starts by saying something like *"This is how I would like you to touch me,"* and then proceeds with a description. If you were doing this with a friend, you would say this as though you were talking to your actual partner.

What if your male partner were to say *"Often, as a guy, I am just not ready to have sex as soon as women seem to want it. Now, I know it is usually the other way around, but I'd just like to get that out in the open and express that that's who I am. I think maybe because I have developed and enhanced the feminine side of myself, I am now more in touch with my need for nurturing and cuddling and loving."*

He might continue, for example, by saying, *"You know I am not like most guys, I really like to spend more time in foreplay. I like for a woman to stroke me all over my body and to kiss me behind my neck and whisper sweet nothings in my ear."*

Well, Wow! For a woman, that would be a wonderful thing for her to hear! But that may not be what the guy says, it might be something entirely different. The fact is you allow both people to say exactly the way they like to be sexually stimulated.

The Excitement Stage

In a practice session with a surrogate partner, you would only *describe*, how you like to build your sexual energy, as you get more excited.

Now, think about it, at this point if you were actually making love, what would you ask your partner to do? You may ask for an adjustment to your original request. For example, a woman usually likes light stroking in the beginning, but when she is aroused she might like the strokes deeper, stronger, and more frequent. So express this in your trial session as well.

If you are doing this at home with your actual partner, if or when you both feel comfortable enough to do so, you might ask permission to touch each other's body in a more sensual way as you demonstrate or "try out" some of the things you are talking about.

Passionate and Highly Aroused Stage

Finally, you get into expressing how you like penetration to be reached. This should include discussion about how long you want different types of stroking, pressure, if you like toys, role-playing, talking dirty, and any variety of things you might reserve for the passionate and highly aroused stage.

Do this process at least once this week: Maybe once with a friend, and/or once with your actual partner. This whole thing might take up to 20 minutes.

Chapter 11:

Understanding Female & Male Multiple Orgasm

The Heart Leaps with Joy When Beloved Partners Merge as One

In order to understand multiple orgasms, it's important to know the essential things that are true for both men and women. Since men and women are physiologically different, especially as concerns the genitals, *and* men tend to have orgasms and ejaculations at the same time, men must work a little harder than women by learning to separate those functions, in order to achieve multi-orgasmic bliss.

Women are naturally multi-orgasmic – it's natural for them to have one orgasm after another without becoming depleted – which happens when a man ejaculates. When men can learn to have multiple orgasms the way women do, without ejaculating, then they can keep pace with women and have almost as much pleasure. At the same time they can experience the reward of becoming more energized instead of becoming energy-depleted.

Who Is Responsible for Your Orgasm? Setting the Record Straight

What is essential in understanding orgasms is to know that basically *you* are the only one responsible for your orgasms. You are responsible for your own orgasms, period. Nobody has to do it to you or for you. Male or female, you need to be the one responsible for yourself.

So, say you are in the process of making love and your partner is not giving you all of what you want because he/she is busy doing something else that you are *really liking*. So what you could do is give *yourself* that other thing you want. Why not? There is an element of excitement and/or naughtiness with touching yourself in front of your partner, and even though women are very shy to do this, and probably men too – it works well, to just push yourself a little, to get past the shyness and get into it. Your partner almost always finds it very erotic when you pleasure yourself so don't deny them the extra pleasure either.

Multiple Orgasm – Exponential Ecstasy
for Men & Women

"The Five Techniques for Multiple Orgasm" Chart Outline

	In Breath	Out Breath
1	Use breath, visualization and intent to Raise sensual energy (root to crown)	Let energy flow from crown to toes and finger tips
2	PC Pump: Tighten/ lift PC muscle to pump up energy along with breath	Release PC Muscle
3	Rotate pelvis up contracting stomach and PC Muscles	Rotate pelvis down releasing muscles (stomach pops out)
4	Breathe up into chest, visualizing breath reaching center of brain	First purr like a Kitten; later building to a loud "Roar" like a lion
5	Vibrate or "shiver" hips to simulate sending orgasmic energy up the spine	"Shiver & *shake it till you make it"* – leads to creating real Orgasmic response and vibratory sounds

The theory and actual performance of each step or phase, is expanded upon below, and for the most part the techniques are the same for both sexes. The man has to be especially careful that he doesn't "go over the top," whereas with the woman, this isn't an issue.

Technique 1:

Breathing

In learning multiple orgasm, you first learn to breathe – with breathing just being a nice deep, even, rhythmic breath – all the way in and all the way out, much like a yoga or meditation breath (or a breath you would use if you were doing martial arts). Initially the breathing should be very slow, to maintain control. The faster a man or woman breathes, the more excited they get, and the faster a man comes. A masterful man can modulate his breath to slow down and/or speed up the pace of his excitement. If he gets ahead of the woman, he can slow down his breathing until she catches up.

While you are learning these techniques, whether practicing on yourself, or with your beloved, it's a good idea to start with slow breathing so you can maintain your focus until the techniques get to be second nature. If you *are* teaching your beloved, *please*, make sure the techniques are already second nature before you attempt this. There is nothing worse than to have your partner reject your idea because you made a sloppy presentation and they don't believe it will work.

In Tantric sexual practice, breathing is an art all to its own. Normally the man and woman breathe in tandem, thus experiencing fine synchronicity between their bodies. This can happen naturally through entrainment, like walking in step, or by consciously breathing together.[23] Opposite breathing is often practiced in the Yab-Yum position.

So let's put it all together now. This process is initially easiest to do standing up. You may want to stand in front of a mirror as you practice these techniques. We'll start with breathing and add each technique, one at a time, until they are all going at once. For the sake of this practice, once all five techniques are going all at once, let's "ramp-up" the energy more quickly, as though we were already a few minutes into it.

Take a long, slow rhythmic breath in while raising your arms up to the top of your head (a reminder to send breath up spine), and then, as you bring hands down to touching toes position, let your breath out. Do a few of these long, slow breaths (in – arms up; out – arms down).

Technique 2:

Sounds to Amplify Sexual Energy

When practicing, it's a good idea, to start with minimal sounds with every breath. What would be the sound you'd make if someone were stroking you somewhere on your body and you like it? How about "Mummm…," the universal sound of expressing pleasure. Every time you breathe out, make the "Mummm…" sound, which I also

---

23 To explain entrainment, I think of a train, where you have the first car moving along and pulling all the cars that follow after it, all doing the same thing. So it's *entraining* your breathing, whether you think about it or not, that gets your breathing in sync with your partner.

call the appreciative sound. When you start practicing with a partner, you both keep up the purring, allowing the sounds to get bigger and bigger as your excitement builds. Eventually, you'll build to giant roars.

If you're a guy, another way you can release sexual energy (to avoid ejaculation) is by letting sound come out of your mouth instead of your lingam. Sound is so important, and yet, here is the place where men are usually the weakest. Because he has been implored since he was a young child to be "strong and silent," he thinks he needs to go through his whole life without ever expressing any emotions. Maybe this is appropriate in the office, but certainly not for the bedroom.

If you've ever watched a porn video, you've probably noticed that the men are the silent ones and the women make all the noise. But honest to Goddess, this is not how the natural man is made. Think more of Tarzan. Now beating your chest and roaring can become part of what you do for yourself and your Jane, to heighten the excitement and amplify the pure joy and fun of gleeful expression.

Sounds wake up your partner and keep you both in touch with your feelings and with what is going on with your body.

That's why it is very, *very* important to make sounds, and continue making them all throughout your lovemaking session. There are lots and lots of different ways to have sounds happen. The sound in the beginning would be a little appreciative sound like mmmmm. What happens when you pet a cat – does the cat go mmmmm? The cat purrs and if you keep petting it the cat will continue purring. That cat isn't embarrassed that it is purring, doesn't care if it is purring or not and doesn't care if *you* know that it is purring.

The cat might be unaware that purring is what happens automatically when it is getting stimulated. Just pretend that you are a cat, in which purring with mmmmmms is highly suggested – you want to continue communicating with your partner by letting him or her know that you're mmmmmmm, appreciating every single part of what is going on.

That way your partner can keep up with your breath and know when you are breathing in and out, hear and feel the pleasure you are having. If you weren't making those sounds, what would your partner do? If you were receiving a stroke from a partner, and the partner doesn't know that you are enjoying it because you are silent, he or she might change the stroke, and you are thinking, *"Hmmm that is interesting, why did she change that stroke I was enjoying so much?"*

If you are really enjoying something you want to let your Partner know. You can let him/her know just by sounds – *"Mmmmmm, ohhhhh, oh that is so good, oh I love that."* It doesn't mean, by the way, if you are a guy and your woman is making these sounds, to do it harder and stronger, like men often do. It means, *that's* the stroke that the woman wants and she wants you to continue doing the stroke *exactly* the way you were doing it when she said she likes it, not to make it harder or deeper or stronger.

I suggest being creative with your vocal chords – playing around with your sounds, being imaginative, making big sounds – especially roaring like a lion, "Roooaaaarrrrrr!" For men, once again, that is a way to divert the energy from coming out of your lingam – instead the energy is coming out of your mouth. So you are tricking your body into diverting its energy so you do not have to ejaculate.

Technique 3:

The PC Pump to Open the Third Eye

Added to the first two techniques, you will be *pumping* your sexual energy up the spine with your breath and intention, by pulling up and contracting the PC or pubococcygeus muscle.

In the introduction to the *"Five Techniques for Multiple Orgasm,"* we talked about the "PC Pump" and how to use it to create more pleasurable orgasms.

Now let's expand on information that will help you to use the PC for greater leverage. This muscle, and a surrounding group of muscles loosely referred to the "PC muscle," is really important in learning how to understand the physiology of orgasms. Orgasms are stronger, better and more pleasurable when your PC muscle is well developed.

How do you find the PC muscle? In a man – and in a woman, too, but in a man it is more obvious – it's the muscle that you pull up on when you stop peeing: You are holding peeing back (or stopping peeing) when you pull up on that muscle. You might notice, if you are a guy, the lingam also moves upwards or at least has a little tug on it when you pull up or tighten-up that muscle. In a woman it's the same thing, you just can't easily see evidence of pulling up on that muscle. If you're a woman, through tightening your PC muscle, it feels as through you are tightening and pulling up your whole pelvic floor.

The simplistic "visual" is that the strongest part of the PC muscle* surrounds the lingam in a man, and the yoni or vagina in a woman, like a "sling." [24]

Get That PC in Shape!

The PC is an essential part of a group of several muscles that form a network of very strong and wide muscles that manage several functions in the pelvic area, including keeping your thrusting powerful, and your orgasms pleasurable.

In anyone who is physically "out of shape" and maybe doesn't eat well or exercise, it's not unusual to have flaccid pelvic muscles. This is also fairly common in older people who have stopped having sex. One extreme side effect can be incontinence.

As a woman, if you have had childbirth training you'd be familiar with "kegel's," a process of tightening and

---

[24] Viewed from the top, the PC is attached to the front to the pubic bone (which is where it gets the "pubo" part of its name). The two halves sweep along the sides of the pelvis and attach at the rear to the coccyx or tail bone. In a side view the PC, is funnel-shaped, with the narrow end facing down, surrounding the rectum/anus.

Seen from above, the PC forms a "U" shape as it wraps around the rectum, and attaches to the coccyx (the "coccy' part of its name which is the coccygeus connection for the PC muscle – which is why it is called "pubo-coccygeus" muscle).

releasing the PC muscle in order to manage the pain of birth-contractions. Childbirth aside, practicing kagels also strengthens the perineum in the vaginal area of women.

In order to strengthen their prostates, now gyms are teaching men kegel's too, to strengthen the prostate. But perhaps most importantly, a strong PC is needed to deepen the sensations of sexual arousal and strength of the orgasm. Needless to say (making the Martial Arts connection which we did starting on page 150), muscle control is extremely important in Karate too.

The Third Eye – Its Relation to Pleasurable Sex Hormones

We have an etheric center in the middle of the forehead (between our brows) which is called the Third-Eye, or Ajna Chakra, and relates to the hormone-producing Pituitary and Pineal glands, emitting the "feel good" hormones, endorphins and oxytocin.[25] This spiritual energy center is also known for enhancing extra sensory perception – clairvoyance,, clairaudience, and clairsentience.

Imagine the intent of having the breath, accompanied by sexual energy you are shooting up your spine with your PC Muscle pump, stimulate the pineal and pituitary glands to release endorphins and oxytocin, ramping up the pleasure you are sending around your body.

---

25 Oxytocin, because it is released during love making, birthing, breastfeeding, and bonding, is often referred to as "The Love Hormone." It helps mammals feel good and prompts nurturing feelings and behavior. Oxytocin is actually produced in the hypo-thalamus and released into the blood through the Pituitary (oxytocin is also produced in the reproductive organs of mammals).

You can roll your eyes up and "looking" back into the center of the brain as you do this, and notice the little "explosions" or fluxuations of white and golden energy that appear like a tiny fireworks on your closed eyelids.

When I look at Picasso's painting, "Sleeping Peasants," in my imagination I am seeing this young couple in state of bliss after making love, with their eyes rolled back in ecstasy, experiencing a state much like I just described above.

While making love in the Yab-Yum position both the man and the woman can stroke their free arm from the coccyx up the spine of their partner to remind them to move their delicious Kundalini sexual energy up the spine on the 'in' breath.

At the top, hold your breath for one second, to the count of one-one-thousand, and then breathe out down the front of the body as you send the energy down to the tips of your toes. Taking this 'second' also reminds you about your breath, which brings you back to the present, each and every breath. On the 'out' breath you can imagine a fountain-like flow of sparkling energy.

If your are standing up and practicing these techniques for the first time, while breathing out your arms follow down to touch the toes. You only do this for the sake of this exercise but not in the actual act of making love. This adds visual understanding of the elongated-oval pathway in which you are sending your energy around the body.

Continue the out-breath up to the bottom of the spine, where the new breath starts, and like before, the PC Pump shoots energy and oxygen up the spine to the top of the head and letting go, allowing the energy to flow back down around the body. In the process of sending a combination of your sexual, chakric, and hormonal energy around this closed-circuit system, you awaken the body into becoming an orgasmic instrument of exponentially increasing pleasure.

When a man is sending his sexual energy around his body, this helps to dissipate the trigger-set tension away from the genitals that can inadvertently create an unwanted ejaculatory release. Additionally, when a man is doing the PC pump, he needs to relax the muscular contractions with each and every out-breath, which also helps to prevent going over the top. It might seem like an oxymoron for a guy to be relaxed at the same time that he is highly aroused and excited, but that's what's necessary to prevent an accident. When the middle of the body is relaxed there's a much better chance of continuing without any mishaps.

Technique 4:

Pelvic Rotation

Once you've gotten a handle on the PC Pump, then add the pelvic rotation to what you're already doing. The pelvis rotates up on the in-breath, and down on the out-breath as follows:

Standing up or lying on a flat surface with your knees bent up and feet hip-width apart, on the in-breath, tightening the stomach muscles, tilt the pelvis up. Make sure that your back is still straight or flat and doesn't rise up with the pelvis. On the out- breath, releasing the stomach muscles, you fully rotate the pelvis the opposite direction, downwards, so that the curvature of the spine is so pronounced that you can insert an arm in the resulting space between the surface you are lying on and the back.

It helps if you can imagine driving a stick-shift car – going from *First gear*, passing through *Neutral* – a flat spine - and straight into *Reverse* on the out-breath.

- On the in-breath, pelvis rotates UP to *First*,

- Back DOWN, through *Neutral*, going straight to *Reverse* on the out-breath,

- back UP on next in-breath, right through *Neutral*, and into *First* again.

If you are familiar with Yoga, this is a little like the pelvis movement in the Cat-Cow pose, but with opposite breathing.

Bigger Sounds

As you simulate higher levels of excitement, the body kicks in and thinks it's having a good time, especially when you add the increasingly more excited sounds like a lion's roar, which I encourage doing at the apex of your excitement. It's worth repeating, that when a man does this, letting BIG energy out of the mouth, he lets off steam that might normally cause a premature ejaculation.

Technique 5:

Shiver & Shake It 'Till You Make It

The techniques include a way that you can shake it 'till you make it. I am not talking about faking orgasms or anything close to that. But what I *am* suggesting is that you teach your body what it feels like when you are having multiple orgasms:

When you have these little vibrations or shivers called "kriyas" that move up your spine in little waves of energy, that is a baby orgasm. Orgasms are pleasurable releases – little shivers caused by orgasmic Kundalini energy pulsing up your spine.

So if you start making your body vibrate and shake and shiver like you are having an orgasm, it fools your body into thinking it is actually having orgasms. It's a little like "the tail wagging the dog" – If the tail wags long enough, the dog thinks it's happy. So starting here, you can actually stimulate your body into initiating its own natural process – that of creating *real* organic multiple orgasms.

Once you have started building sexual energy, you can simulate orgasms by shivering and shaking your hips on the out-breath. Little shivers running up the spine may not seem very significant when they first start, but stay with it, and notice that the shivers turn into bigger and bigger shakes, vibrating up the spine, in orgasmic waves of pleasure on both the in and out breath. Initially, real orgasms usually are small and infrequent. Maybe in your next practice session they will get bigger.

In the case of a man, it is very important to NOT ejaculate in practice sessions. This is the best way he can build the "muscle" he needs to discern where that exact place is where he holds back the ejaculation but lets the orgasmic shivers release up his spine. He has to be patient until this happens, or he will never learn. Usually when he is the most excited, just before the place where he would normally ejaculate, is where he can have non-ejaculatory orgasms, i.e., multiple orgasms.

Simulating the Body in a High State of Arousal and Passion

These five techniques, when done all together, actually simulate the body when it's in a high state of arousal and passion. When done right, you actually have complete control over your body. In the case of a man, if his body is galloping ahead without any control at all, the result is premature ejaculation – by far the most common sexual dysfunction. Now he can relax, knowing *he* is the one in control, by orchestrating each of these techniques, and deftly modulating his breathing, sounds, and the pace at which his love-making progresses.

Streaming Sexual Energy Up Through the Spine

One of the main concepts of multiple orgasms is learning to *stream* these waves of delicious energy. Initially it wouldn't be sexual energy, but eventually it would build to sexual energy, up through the core of the body and then back down again in this big oblong kind of circle. This way you are having a circular flow of energy – waves of sensuality flowing continuously through your body, like a closed electrical circuit.

The circuit only opens long enough to input more heightened sexual energy from your second chakra as it is added to the existing energy now flowing up. When the energy reaches the Third Eye area, there's another input of energy from your hormonal glands, but still maintaining the closed circuit concept. This creates an almost exponential increase of pleasure as your breath continues around the circuit. This closed-circuit flow of energy is the thing that you start with, continue, and end with.

Even when you are all done, continue to allow these waves of energy to stream through your body in a restful state of orgasmic bliss for at least 5 or 10 minutes. In a David Deida Tantra class of that I once attended, he asked, "Why is it that men love to ejaculate so much?" His tongue-in-cheek answer, "Because when it is all over, he can finally stop thinking" – a welcome relief from a continuously busy mind.

Consciously Moving Your Kundalini Energy

Once you understand the concept of consciously moving energy, and you have all the techniques down to second nature, this energy can now be your best friend, because it keeps you in touch with how you're experiencing your sensuality and your sexuality while you are making love.

Using the 5 Multi-Orgasmic Techniques in Sacred Union with Your Beloved

Breathing to Get Back in Sync

Let me give you an example of how you might use breathing to get back in sync with your lover:

> *"Honey, you know what? I kind of think we're a little bit out of sync. And it would be great if we could do 'breathing in sync.' So we'll both breathe in and out at the same time, and if I make little sounds while I am breathing it will help. It will notify you of what's going on. So what I would suggest is, that we breathe in, and then as we are breathing out, we will make this little sound that I call the "appreciative" sound (mmmmmm). OK?*
>
> *If you are always making a little mmmm when you breathe out, then I can hear you and I know we are breathing together and we can focus on breathing together. Another thing is, your breath is a little deeper and longer than mine, and mine is a little bit shorter than yours, so let's just try to balance that out so that we are breathing in tandem or in sync."*

Using Opposite-Breathing with the Yab-Yum

Your partner's response to the above might be:

> *"Oh, that sounds great. And you know what I would like to try? I would like to try something that I have heard is very effective – when we do the Yab-Yum position, my legs are crossed and you would be sitting on my lap, facing me, with your legs wrapped around my middle. From here I would like to try doing 'opposite breathing' – so as you are breathing in, I am breathing out, and as we rotate our pelvises, our bodies will 'wave' in this sort of wave-form flow of energy going up our spines.*
>
> *We can help each other move energy up the spine like this: I will hold your back with one arm and raise my free hand up the back of your spine to remind you to move your energy up. During this 'opposite breathing' our bodies can do the opposite motions – with opposite movement of the hips as well. I would just love to try that."*

I hope these examples will stimulate you're thinking of more creative and compassionate ways to let your partner know what you'd like to try.

Being in the Now Through Breathing Can Stimulate Orgasms

The next most important thing that both partners need to know is how to be "in the now" – the present. The breath really helps to do that. Without breathing you may not stay at the point where you are both completely here *now*, available, ready, listening, and in tune with the other person. I once had a couple as clients, a husband and wife who came to me, and the woman was not having orgasms during penetration. She could have orgasms with a vibrator, but when they were making love she couldn't have orgasms.

So, I taught them both *"The Five Techniques for Multiple Orgasm."* Somewhere in that process I was coaching her husband in how to touch his wife and what to do, step by step, and suddenly she had an enormous breakthrough – a vaginal orgasm that neither one of them anticipated.

It was a huge, wonderful, great, passionate orgasm that just rocked her whole body. She was so excited and happy and so was her husband. After it was all over, I asked her, *"What was the single thing that seemed to make the most difference?"*

And she said, *"Hands down, it was the breath. Breathing like that kept me right here, kept me focused, kept my mind from wandering around and getting off center, and that's why it worked for me."*

So if you think that breathing is just, oh, *"Well, if I didn't breathe I would be dead,"* that *is,* in fact, what *I* used to think – that "learning" breathing isn't all that important because we do it automatically. I was wrong. Learning these techniques will change your whole outlook on breath, because conscious breathing keeps you in the present.

If you are in the present it allows you perception of the little nuances of the moment. The gift (or the present) once again, is where you need to be. If you are not in the moment, maybe it's because you have an agenda – you're racing ahead to accomplish your agenda, and then what happens?

You miss the moment. You miss that wonderful little moment that could have happened that could have thrown you both into total ecstasy. So don't be in a hurry, be willing to breathe, stay with that person, match their energies, and be connected – especially connected through the heart and with your gaze into each other's eyes.

Pacing and Keeping the Energy Up

Sometimes in lovemaking you find that you are both going at it, and something's missing. It might be that what's missing, energetically, is one or both of you, is out of sync with the other person. So at this point (which I have mentioned several times), you might say to your partner, *"You know things just aren't working for me the way that I would like them to – I feel like we are racing ahead. I don't have any goals to accomplish here and I would just like to slow down a little bit."*

Or, *"I would just like to stop and give you a really delicious melting hug, and just sit or lie here and cuddle with you for the moment."* Those are ways to modulate the energy, and then restart, getting the pace going so you are both together on the same track again.

Often the energy might be moving a little slow and you might do some conscious things to speed it up, like breathing faster – or consciously moving hips and breathing faster, or giving more attention to the techniques for multiple orgasm and really focusing on those until you get your energy back up to speed.

Taking a Man to Heaven Through Female Multiple Orgasm

A man starts feeling in his sex chakra and works up to his heart. A woman starts feeling in her heart chakra and works down to the sex organs.

Obviously, the female physiology is different than the male. A man initially starts feeling open or aroused in his sexual center through connecting with his lover, and finally raises his energy up to open his heart.

A woman first opens her heart, and this helps her to feel safe. At this point, she can proceed to arousal and then to desire. We talked about how a man goes from 0 - 60 in about ten seconds and a woman takes much, much longer. In actuality, a man can have an ejaculation fairly quickly, like within say, 3 to 7 minutes. I think 15 minutes is the national average for making love – if you could call *that* lovemaking.

I don't know how you can actually demonstrate a lot of lovemaking in seven minutes. For me, I am happy with several hours of lovemaking. That's why I like practicing the techniques for multiple orgasms – that allows both the man and the woman to spend a lot longer having sex without the man ejaculating and having to stop. Pleasure increases exponentially the longer a couple makes love, until they become one with the Tantric wave of Pleasure, a rarefied merging with Divine ecstasy.

Amrita – the Female Equivalent of Ejaculation

By the way, I have found that a woman can, even if she does ejaculate, do it over and over again whereas for a man it is quite different. A woman does not have to build up a lot of testosterone to be able to have her equivalent female ejaculation – Amrita. Because some women *do* experience Amrita, it is important for them to know that they can continue to have more and more squirting or gushing, as it is often called, without having to stop and start over. Most men can't do this. So, this is another very important way that women are different than men.

The Sensual Woman's Body Needs Foreplay

Perhaps the most important difference is that a woman can get so much into the sensuality of her body that she begins to feel like every place she is touched is an erogenous zone. So if a guy understands that about a woman, he will spend a lot of time touching or stroking her before they get into the body of sexual activity.

It might mean a massage, it might mean stroking, it might mean cuddling – and that could go on for 10 or 15 minutes, a half hour, or whatever that woman needs. A guy has got to understand that this is part of the process.

We could call that foreplay – an essential part of awakening a woman that lets her know that she is in a body – that lets her start to feel her body all over before moving into the genital area.

Establishing a Protocol to Keep a Man From Going Over the Top

Something a woman might initiate is setting a protocol for ensuring that her partner doesn't release prematurely. The protocol could be, that when her partner starts to reach "maximum arousal," that he gives her some kind of signal, where she would know when to "pull back." The signal could just be for the man to say "stop!" This way she doesn't *over-arouse* her partner and send him right over the top.

Because a man is so easily and quickly excited, it's not a good idea for a woman to start by seriously stroking her man's lingam until she herself, has had quite a bit of touching from him. Neither one of you wants him to unexpectedly release.

When Is It the Right Time for Penetration?

The guy needs to know to wait for penetration until his lover is begging for more. Before a man starts genital touching, or before going on to the next phase, the man has to know when his partner is ready. He might *think* she is ready, but if she's not begging, he better not go there.

What do I mean by begging? She might be wiggling and moving her body around and panting and breathing heavily and going, *"Uhh, oh that feels so good."* That doesn't mean she is ready to go to the next stage.

So what you need to do is ask her *"Would you like me to touch your clitoris, honey?"* – To which she might respond, *"Well, no I am not quite ready for that but I will be in a minute or two."*

Another example, *"So, darling, don't you think it would be great if I inserted my lingam into your beautiful, juicy yoni?"*

"Oh it is a wonderful idea, but not quite yet darling, I am not quite ready for that."

So asking is the best way to find out if a woman really, *really* wants you to go to the next stage. You could have little signals you set up. If a woman is very close to her lover, she could say, "When I start biting your ear that means I am ready for insertion." Or choose whatever signal you both decide on if you don't want to have to talk about it.

If in doubt, another common practice, is for the woman to just take the man by his lingam and put him inside her. But, in rare exceptions, the man may not be ready. So even though a man is a little bit more obvious than a woman, she should probably ask him too. Asking is very important and certainly the right thing to do: *"Is it ok if I do this now darling?"*

Here's the Part About Going to Heaven

Once the woman is having one multiple orgasm after another, her excitement, wildness and capacity for pleasure will pull her multi-orgasmic man right into the flow of the *Tantric Wave of Pleasure*, as they go to higher and higher levels of bliss. Finally they merge with the river of Divine Ecstasy flowing continually through them, their bodies vibrating and quivering with pleasure, so much so that every cell of their bodies have become an orgasmic instrument of pleasure.

Male Multiple Orgasm - Different Strokes for Different Folks

In male multiple orgasms, we are not talking about multiple ejaculations, but only about the orgasmic sensations that can be released without ejaculation. Once he learns how, a man can have lots of orgasms, pleasurable releases more like a woman's orgasms, without ejaculating. Learning *The Five Techniques for Multiple Orgasm* solves the problem of premature ejaculation. Women love it when men can do this, because they can have lots of multiple orgasms together, thus "amping-up" the level of excitement between them.

It is not always a bad thing for a guy to go over the top, if he is say, between the ages of 15 and 35. Younger men have high testosterone levels and are highly excitable. Testosterone provides the makings of sperm, and having lots of it makes a young man able to have one ejaculation after another. The reasoning behind having fewer ejaculations, to preserve strength, hardness, and a continuing ability to "keep it up" is often lost on the young guy, who doesn't care, because he can get it up again almost immediately.

But after age 35 he is not as likely to have another erection. In fact his ejaculation is more than likely to put him to sleep. Too many women, who are all ready to go again, are disappointed to find their partner snoozing. Unfortunately, this is due to the physiological lessening of testosterone levels, steadily decreasing over age 35.

On the other hand, there *are* a few blessed older guys who don't have that as a restriction or a limitation, regardless of their age – they can keep coming and starting over again.

But I think, in general, for most men, they pretty much follow the patterns just described.

Prolonging the Pre-Ejaculatory Stage

How long of an orgasmic interlude can you have prior to the man ejaculating? If practiced in the *"Five Techniques to Multiple Orgasm,"* a man can last indefinitely, but realistically speaking, maybe 4 or 5 hours. After all, Sting said he takes 9 hours making love to his wife, Trudie. Yum!

The pre-ejaculatory stage goes right up to the place where a man feels like he is almost ready to come, and in his mind, it is a matter of keeping it at that place where he is so excited that he feels he is just about to go over the top, but *doesn't.*

He just keeps it right there, in that state where he feels, *"Oh, I feel like I am almost coming, I am almost coming, I am almost coming, I am almost coming, I am almost coming, I am almost coming,"* and this just goes on ad infinitum, where he keeps it right there, but never actually comes.

It is at that stage, he can actually have his multiple orgasms. So when he gets to the place where he can say, *"I am almost coming,"* – that's where he wants to hold back the ejaculation and allow the orgasms to continue up through his body, to wave up his spine, shivering and shaking in little kriyas that rise upward, bringing the sexual energy up to the third eye, activating the pituitary and pineal glands, and sending the resultant endorphins down through the rest of the body in this continuous oval circle in which he is recycling and multiplying this delicious sexual energy streaming around his body.

Having Multiple Orgasms — A Little Like a Fireworks Display

When a guy recognizes what a little, tiny, baby orgasm feels like as he releases it up his spine, he is on his way to more and bigger multiple orgasms (remember the "Piss Shiver" in which there is no ejaculation?).

Imagine that his first few little pleasurable "multiple orgasms" are comparable to a fireworks display – they are

like the first few firecrackers that go off at the beginning of a show – mostly small and insignificant ones. Then there is a break and a few more, slightly bigger ones go off. Then another break and soon there are several more, bigger and more spectacular. This continues for the next hour

or so until the time for the grand finale arrives. This is comparable to when a man ejaculates – Hundreds of fireworks are released all at once! Bang! Bang! Bang! And then it's all over.

Many older Tantric men choose to avoid the "grand finale" to save that precious testosterone for the next time they want to get it up. They've had a great time all night with many, many pleasurable orgasms. Why blow it all at the end?

I've noticed that by not coming, when a man decides he's had enough, he can rest and feel the delicious endorphins and pleasurable sensations from his orgasms coursing through his body, still quivering and shivering for a long time after his activity has stopped. This alone, is reason enough to lie in a meditative state, breathing, and still quietly moving the energy around in the big oval with his breath, as he relaxes and enjoys this state of bliss. Too bad that David Deida didn't include this in his reasons for why a man likes to come so much, but of course, multiple orgasms aren't technically "coming."

These pleasurable sensations often last for a couple of hours, and then again maybe, when he wakes up, those shivery orgasmic sensations might *still* be hanging around.

Increasingly Blissful Plateaus of Pleasurable Vibrations

Now getting back to when a couple is making love: A man can make multiple orgasms last for hours, if he wants to. Of course, he won't be able to hold that stage of "almost coming" excitement forever, because there is an ebb and flow to every stage of making love. This might mean going through a period of multiple orgasms and then a leveling out, which I call "plateauing" out. Then there would be another period of multiple orgasms, in which, hopefully, both partners would be having multiple orgasms together (but not necessarily), and then leveling out at the next plateau.

So each time you both level out at a higher plateau, then an even higher plateau, and finally you get to the place where you absolutely are in tune, or tuned in to what I call the "Tantric Wave of Pleasure." In this rarified atmosphere you are tapping in to the ecstasy and blissfulness of the divine energy that you are now open to, as though you were tuning it in on a radio dial and you are suddenly now in the wave of pleasure. It is going through your body like a river, flowing through you. Your whole body is vibrating and quivering with pleasure and orgasmic shaking and shivering. It gets to the point where the energy gets so very high and exciting you almost don't need to be touching each other's body, and don't even need to be actually sexually engaged for this to continue happening. So this is what is possible to experience after enough time – going through these different phases and merging into that orgasmic wave of pleasure – the Tantric Wave of Pleasure. Most Earth beings don't even know that the possibility of having this much ecstasy exists.

Guys Don't Always Have to Think About Performing, Really!

One last thing about a guy thinking that he has to perform: **Guys do not have to perform**. Even though you think you have to, you don't have to always keep thinking about keeping your lingam hard. It doesn't always have to be hard and erect. You can just go with the ebb and the flow. When the time is right it gets hard again quite naturally. You don't really have to keep it hard all the time, guys. Really.

Sometimes, if you are too excited and your lingam is throbbing with anticipation, your partner might not be ready for that – that degree of intensity at that time. In this case it has to be okay for you to go soft, or for your excitement to wilt and for different things to happen around your lingam and you still don't have to worry about it. It is always going to come back.

All a guy needs to do, is to keep the energy running through his body (which takes the pressure to ejaculate off of his genital area) and it's okay if this works *too* well if he gets a little bit soft, or it is not as hard as he would like it to be, he *still* doesn't have to perform. There is plenty of time for that. As long as he is relaxed and you're both in sync eventually everything is going to work out the way it should.

Don't think about where you're going, or when you're going to ejaculate or how you are going to make it happen, or how to keep it hard all the time – that is not where you need to keep your head, guys. All you need to do is just be present. All you need to do is just focus on your breathing and enjoying your partner.

This is not about being the biggest, baddest, strongest or first to cross the "finish" line. But rather about enjoying and appreciating every step of the journey that doesn't seemingly go anywhere. All the while you're having a great time merging with your partner.

Merge and create magic together where the whole is greater than the sum of the parts, where the energy between you opens up to God-like dimensions of ecstasy beyond human comprehension.

Chapter 12:
The Many Ways to Please Your Partner

True Pleasure Comes From Expressing Our Divine Sacred Hearts

In learning about the many ways to please your partner, I would like to introduce you to the "Five Pleasure Centers."

The Five Pleasure Centers

The First Pleasure Center

The most obvious pleasure center is the sex chakra, in which pleasure is a natural occurrence when one gets stimulated genitally. This is the part of the body we usually jump to when we think about pleasure, or sexual pleasure – especially for men, but for women too. I've noticed in working with hundreds of clients over the years, that there are several other pleasure centers, though none so obvious as the genital area.

The Second Pleasure Center

The body itself, especially the organ of the skin, which covers the whole outside of the body, is very sensitive to touch. We love the sensations of being touched and stroked.

Moving deeper into the body with massage – into the muscles and deep into the fleshy parts of the body can be very, very pleasurable and often orgasmic. Touching, feeling the skin, and "toning" (vibrating tones into the body, or body parts) can greatly enhance one's lovemaking experience.

Imagine that you're making tones directly with your mouth on your partner's stomach, with sounds like *"mwo mwo mwo mwo mwo mwa"* or other sounds that are fun and stimulating. Those sounds/vibrations go directly into the body through the skin and enhance one's overall experience of pleasure.

Remember that during sexual activity, the body is capable of becoming an orgasmic instrument of pleasure, which cinches it as the second pleasure center.

The Third Pleasure Center

Now, this may seem a little bit wacky, but I'd like to introduce the heart-mind combination. When you're experiencing loving-pleasure, it's the combination of the heart and the mind together. Recent scientific evidence is proving that the heart actually thinks. The heart may be the "smarter" of the two because it thinks with feelings of compassion and love.

The mind thinks in a different way than the heart – the mind is more analytical and the heart is more feeling – somewhat analogous to the difference between the left and right brain.

We receive so much of our stimulation through being turned-on visually, which is why Playboy Magazine is so popular. If a beautiful woman or attractive man walks into the room, both women and men notice – a response that happens in the brain.

Typically, when you combine the heart and the mind together, you have both the knee-jerk response of the brain to visual and associative sexual stimuli, as well as an opening of the heart, bringing in the love component. When these elements are combined, you are experiencing the third pleasure center – the heart and mind connection, which can be absolutely divinely pleasurable, especially as you begin to trust and open to feelings of the heart.

The Fourth Pleasure Center

In spiritual terms, the third eye has to do with the "will," and extra-sensory perception (ESP). Additionally it is synonymous with the physical center of the brain, where the endocrine gland production of important sexual hormones like beta-endorphins and oxytocin takes place. Using the PC Pump, to deliver oxygen and sexual energy to these glands, and activating their release through intention, we now have feel-good hormones circulating through the body due to the Fourth Pleasure Center, the third eye chakra.

The Fifth Pleasure Center

Without openness to the crown chakra, the third-eye would just be an element of will. If the will defers to your higher self (represented by the crown chakra at the top of the head), the resulting intuition and guidance can make you into a powerful force.

Opening your will to accepting the guidance of the higher self can also help you to experience the transcendent awareness of Samadhi – becoming one with the Divine infinite state of ecstasy.

Experiencing this state is the Fifth Pleasure Center, which is not really "in" the body, but the body is "in" it. When this experience happens we have tapped in or tuned in, to the Divine realm of pleasure.

Divine ecstasy and bliss is there for us to access at any time. Finding this pleasurable state is like tuning into a radio frequency – it's always there but if you don't dial in to the exact right notch you won't get the station.

Whether it is through meditation, through sex, or in this case using the *Five Techniques for Multiple Orgasm*, we are consciously tuning in to that wave of Divine ecstasy, through being in the now, being one with Source, being one with our partner, and merging through our pleasure centers. When these waves of pleasure start to

flow though us, they are hard to stop. In the act of physical union, you can keep going, reaching new levels of more and more pleasure, to a point that you don't even need to be physically touching each other to continue experiencing the waves of pleasure coursing through your body.

The best way to activate the fifth center is to set your intentions at the beginning of lovemaking and then forget about them as you merge with your partner. When giving and receiving pleasure from your beloved, by simply focusing on the breath and going with the flow, you can stay open to the nuances of the moment – not having an agenda can take you to becoming one with the infinite state of ecstasy.

So now that you know about the five pleasure centers, you can see that euphoria doesn't have come in just one package. We can be sexually excited or turned-on in many delightful ways. By combining those five pleasure centers you can have rapture beyond your wildest dreams.

God and Goddess Spots

How the Male Prostate and Female G-Spot Stimulation Are Similar

When people are engaging sexually, they seldom give attention to the male sacred-spot and the female g-spot, which is a shame, because done correctly, g-spot stimulation produces the maximum of pleasure for both men and women. Surprisingly enough, the techniques used are very similar for both sexes. A man's scared-spot can be accessed through the anal canal near the pubic bone. The woman's g-spot is essentially in the same location but in her vaginal canal.

A Practical Mudra ²⁶

The one mudra, or finger position, that works particularly well for both male and female g-spot massage, is using the middle finger (slightly crooked forward as though you were making a "come hither" gesture), to perform a variety of strokes.

The most common one might be a long vertical up-and-down stroke, across the sacred-spot or g-spot. For a man this stroke would be used while simultaneously pumping the lingam, with similar long up and down strokes.

It is also very pleasurable for a woman to get both spots stimulated simultaneously. My favorite clitoral stimulation is done with long strokes: Think of the fingers as being like a railroad track between the clitoris by running two fingers vertically up on either side of the well-lubricated clitoris with a long, slow, deep stroke, pushing the clitoris up

26 Mudras, or hand gestures (a nonverbal means of communication), can range inmeaning from simple aesthetic ornamentation to being a symbolic or ritual gesture, depicting the nature and function of the deity (in Hinduism and Buddhism). Mudras are often used by Tantrikas to communicate knowledge to their adepts or followers. They are also used in dancing as part of a complex vocabulary of the expression of feeling and narrative...

between your fingers. Move the fingers back down again with a firm but softer stroke, and then continue with the same deeper up-stroke. By the way, my favorite lubricant is simply raw, organic coconut oil. It's healthy for you and tastes good too.

It's also important to vary your strokes. One of the most pleasurable strokes is to vibrate your finger on a woman's g-spot, or a man's g-spot. And of course if you are vibrating a finger inside, you want to be vibrating both inside and outside at the same time. By varying these two stokes, the long ones and the vibrational ones, you can go back and forth between them, until or unless your partner asks for something different or you feel the need for a change.

A lingam can also be inserted in the woman's yoni and used the same way as in manually touching that spot, and again, switching between the long and vibrational stroking. While receiving g-spot stimulation in this way, a woman may want to take a turn at pleasuring her own clitoris, as she knows best what to do while her partner is busy thrusting. The same is true for a man to help take part in *his* own pleasure.

A-Spot Orgasms and the U-Spot — New Phenomena?

There's been some recent buzz about two new erogenous zones in a woman, the A-Spot, and the U-Spot, both of which have historically been contacted during lovemaking, creating pleasurable or orgasmic response, but formerly unnamed. Well now they have names, and here is a brief description of each one:

Simpler to understand, lets start with the U-spot: It's a small patch of sensitive erectile tissue located just above and on either side of the urethral opening, forming an upside-down "U" (but doesn't extend below the urethra to the small area between the urethra and the vagina). If you want to see a very detailed photo of this area, please refer to this link: http://womenshealthinwomenshands.org/Images/Anatomy/12ant.jpg

Because it is less well known than the clitoris, American clinical research workers only recently investigated its erotic potential. They found that if this region was gently caressed, with the finger, the tongue, or the tip of the penis, there was an unexpectedly powerful erotic response.

Stimulation of the A-Spot (AFE-zone or Anterior Fornix Erogenous Zone) also called the cul-de-sac, is known to increase orgasmic response, and typically is reached by penile stimulation or a special AFE vibrator (long, thin and upward curved at its end) to probe this zone.

During intercourse, if the penis thrusts deeply enough, it will reach a patch of sensitive tissue at the innermost point of the vagina — an area around the anterior fornix and cul-de-sac, into which the cervix extends. The cervix of the uterus is the narrow part that protrudes slightly into the vagina, leaving a circular recess around itself. Attention to this area can make a woman have "vaginal orgasms."

To make a woman orgasm through her A-Spot, penetration from behind works best. One man says, "Go in as deep as possible and at slightly different angles. Wait until you reach what feels like a little pocket covering your penis head, and continue steady, hard penetration for a few minutes. Keep up this steady penetration until she has an orgasm."

Another man said this as well: "Ever since I have been able to hit this spot, she has experienced the deepest and most satisfying orgasms of her entire life."

Amrita - the Golden Nectar of a Woman

If inner and outer stimulation happens long enough for a woman, it most likely will produce a vaginal orgasm with female ejaculate known as Amrita. Amrita or Amrit, is often called Nectar of the Goddess, or Golden Nectar. It is also referred to in ancient scriptures as the *"drink of the gods granting them immortality."* Amrita is also used to refer to the Universal Womb, the Matrix of Generation and the Source of All.

When a woman has Amrita, it is the most pleasurable, amazing sensation she can experience.[27] It is also amazing for a man to experience a woman having Amrita because he gets drawn into and entrained to her undeniably heightened pleasure.

By the way, this fluid has a totally different composition than a man's sperm. Long ago, it was thought to be urine, but this is not the case. Lab tests show traces of urine, but it is its own unique fluid particular to women.

---

27 Female ejaculate (also known colloquially as squirting or gushing) is a fluid that is expelled from the woman's body through the paraurethral ducts and urethra during orgasm. It originates from the Skene's gland or what some refer to as the female prostate gland.

Maximum Pleasure for Both Men & Women

When a man is receiving simultaneous stroking on both his lingam and his Sacred Spot (male G-Gpot or God-Spot) – that can give *him* the highest level of pleasure that he might experience as well. This is one way that g-spots are very similar both for men and women. Sometimes men like their sacred-spot massaged separately from their lingam. The same is true for singular attention on a woman's g-spot without the clitoral stimulation – but I would say that this is more the exception than the rule. Simultaneous stimulation of *both* areas is the best way to give a man or a woman maximum pleasure.

The Man's God-Spot (Also known as the Male G-Spot and the Sacred Spot)

Most men love a prostate massage. From the inside, the prostate can be found adjacent to the wall of the anal canal. It can be recognized by a soft,  but obvious lump about as big as a soft prune. From the outside, the prostate is opposite the perineum.

Unless the two of you have already built a lot of excitement, you wouldn't want to attempt entering your man's anal canal to find the sacred spot. I personally have found that a man doesn't enjoy being touched on his sacred spot until he's had moderate to extensive stimulation on his lingam.

Your partner usually wants you to keep that dual stimulation going from the beginning to the end. That way he can associate the pleasure that he is already used to, with what might otherwise feel somewhat strange. Done by itself, stimulation of the sacred spot may not be well received – it may seem too much like a doctor's exam that didn't feel particularly good.

If you are performing entry into finding the sacred spot, I suggest using a latex glove and lots of lubricant, and with your middle finger very slowly start penetrating the anus. I call this "knocking at the door." At the entry point is the first sphincter muscle, which you encourage your partner to relax as much as possible. Gentle tapping on that spot makes him aware of letting go there. Immediately after, you'll encounter another sphincter muscle, which can be relaxed in the same way. Once both sphincters are relaxed, you can slowly and easily move your finger up as far in as it can go. If your partner "clamps up" on your finger, keep reminding him to relax those muscles. Now, with that "come hither" gesture, crooking your finger forward towards yourself, you will find the prostate.

Keeping your finger firmly on that spot without moving, ask him "Do you feel my finger on your prostate?" Once he can feel and relax into it, then slowly start stroking up and down, asking him how this feels. Keep communicating, asking what changes he would like and the amount of pressure that feels good.

The prostate gland initially feels soft, but when stimulated (similar to the female g-spot), becomes tighter and "ridgey" (like the area on the roof of your mouth) which differentiates it from the rest of the canal's soft, slippery surrounding tissue.

It's not unusual to feel spasms or pulsations from the prostate, indicating a heightened sense of excitement, which I liken to multiple orgasms. And indeed, your man can be guided to send these vibratory sensations up his spine into the third eye area (discussed in more detail in the section on Shivering & Shaking, pg. 220).

You are likely to find that juices are excreted into this area, indicating increasing arousal, which is why the male g-spot massage is sometimes referred to as *"milking"* the prostate. I jokingly ask my partner how it feels to be penetrated like a woman. Then I remind him that this experience makes him aware of his male/female duality – a helpful realization on the road to enlightenment.

The most effective strokes are a long "up and down" milking-stroke, varied with a pulsing/vibrational stroke. Going back and forth between these two methods builds more excitement. Because this stroking is done simultaneously with stroking the lingam with your other hand, you would preferably be matching strokes.

Continue asking him what he prefers, how much pressure he wants, how often he likes a change of stroke, and when he wants you to keep it the same. Continual verbal communication is the best way to make sure he is receiving pleasure.

As the prostate becomes tighter and more ridgey, it also becomes hotter and hotter. When it gets really, *really* hot – poker hot – this means that he is seconds away from ejaculating. So when you reach that point (if it's not too late already), and he wants to prolong this experience, you might want to stop your motion entirely so he doesn't go over the top. Of course he always has the option to come.

The Woman's Goddess-Spot

Next, let's address pleasuring a woman's g-spot or goddess-spot, which, surprisingly enough, is done in exactly the same way as for a man, and except for being in a different canal, it would be hard to find many differences.

Although most women also love a goddess-spot massage, I would never approach a woman's g-spot until she's had plenty of clitoral stimulation and is already excited. She must be squirming and wiggling and begging for you to go inside before you massage her g-spot.

A woman's g-spot is found just inside the yoni (the woman's vaginal opening), and in just about the same way you would find a man's g-spot, only it's in the vaginal canal and isn't as far in as a man's god-spot. It's found a little above the entrance to the yoni, an inch or two in and just above

the pelvic bone. To make it easy to find, imagine connecting an energetic circle between the thumb on the clitoris and the middle finger on the g-spot.

Same as with a man, you would crook your middle finger up a little towards the pelvic bone in a "come hither" gesture, until you feel the ridgey "roof of your mouth" feeling

251

which gets more pronounced as excitement builds. The "spot" is usually bigger than a silver dollar. When excited, it feels really different from the rest of the tissue in the vagina, which is soft, slippery and wet feeling.

When you find that spot, you want to put steady deep, but gentle pressure on it, until the consciousness of the woman receiving, is drawn down to that spot. She feels her goddess-spot very distinctly different from the rest of her vagina, and by pushing down on and holding that spot, she will eventually feel a lot of pleasure. At this point you might ask her, "Now that you can feel the pressure on your goddess-spot, would you like me to start stroking it?" And if she says, "Yes," you can start stroking her g-spot with long vertical strokes. It's essential to keep in verbal communication with your lover, asking her how she is likes the pressure, the stroking, the vibration, the speed, etc.

If you are giving, you might modulate the pressure to discern where she feels the most pleasure. Try using the same variety of strokes you use in creating clitoral pleasure, simultaneously on the goddess spot. Just as with most men, for most women it makes a big difference in her receptivity to pleasure if she experiences simultaneous massage of the g-spot *and* clitoris together – and by the way, using the same strokes as a man likes.

The first time I ever experienced a g-spot massage I was in my first Tantra workshop, being facilitated by Lori Grace Star and Robert Frey. Although there was no sexual activity during the classes, we could choose to try some of the techniques discussed in class on our own during the lunch break. I asked a married couple there to assist, if they would help me to locate and stimulate my g-spot.

The husband was stroking my breasts and body, and his wife, after working on my clitoris for a while, started stimulating my g-spot. But at that point, no one was stimulating my clitoris. Some women don't need both so it didn't occur to the couple helping me to do that.

I kept waiting to feel the pleasure, but all I felt was pressure, and kind of an uncomfortable feeling in tandem with an urge to pee. When I mentioned that sensation, they said "Not to worry, this is normal – you don't really need to pee." Then a few minutes later I suddenly felt a tightening followed by involuntary contractions resulting in squirting a stream of Amrita straight up to the ceiling.

The couple felt quite pleased with their accomplishment and congratulated me for achieving orgasm through my g-spot. I was amazed, because I didn't feel any pleasure at all!

It was only later that I realized that for me, the combination of simultaneous stimulation of both the g-spot and the clitoris is an absolute necessity to feel the pleasure. Now it's hard *not* to feel pleasure, because done this way, the g-spot enhances my orgasmic capacity exponentially.

I especially like the vibrational pulsation pushing deeply on my g-spot with like pressure on my clitoris, but I can only take it for short periods of time. By going back to the long back-and-forth stroking, and varying these two strokes, I easily have many, many orgasms.

In Closing

Now that you have read this book, I would like to summarize the journey we have been through together – hopefully arm in arm with your partner.

Healing with Communication & Creating Intimacy by Enhancing Your Heart Connection

I hope that you have already started to implement the tools made available in "HE♥RTGASM!," that help you to avoid arguments, the most important of which is Compassionate Communication (aka NVC). Please don't under estimate the power of this great tool and *use it as often as possible,* especially when things start heading south. The quicker you can detect that a clash is imminent, the easer it is to look inside and start expressing your feelings in order to divert things from escalating to into a brawl.

If you are a couple, I also hope that you are already having your weekly withholds meetings at a set day and time. If so, I'm sure you are finding this a really valuable tool in preventing misunderstandings and disconnects.

Finally, have you set up your weekly evening to spend several hours on yourselves alone, freeing you to have a wonderful, sensual time to giggle, play, romp and make love together?

This is so essential in the busy lives of couples with children, and if you aren't doing this now, please don't let this precious time drift away, and like so many others, wake up when the children are gone and wonder why your relationship has lost its fire.

Embracing Love by Starting Within – with Yourself –and Then Going for the Highest Good for All

Have you begun to realize your own spiritual nature –your connection to your higher self? I hope so, because this sets you on a direct path to loving your self as the magnificent spiritual being that you already are. Now from within, you can "be" the love you have been seeking outside of yourself.

I sincerely hope you have tried the Instant Light Meditation, because as much an oxymoron as this may sound, it's truly possible get instantly centered by just taking a few moments to refocus and get back to business refreshed and inspired!

Realizing a higher purpose is part of the mindset that is required to make the shift from an ordinary relationship, into one of a loving, in-tune, and vibrant alliance.

If you and your partner have acknowledged that you can break the ego-habit of always having to be right, you are indeed on the path to a union that works. Have you begun to honor the uniqueness of your beloved? Do you allow them be "alright just as they are," and have it be okay to live with different points of view?

If you're doing this, you can now more readily agree to disagree, which often helps the two of you to see eye-to-eye where it really matters. It's great when neither partner is ever made to feel that they *have* to do something on the behalf of the other.

Perhaps the most important mindset in this book is the concept of going for the higher greatest good. This allows for the freedom every person wants as an individual in a partnership, while at the same time, having the motivation to please and be of service because of the high level of love and respect that it engenders in each other.

Attracting the Love You Want, Bypassing Power Struggles & Creating Pleasure Through Energy Dynamics

The other really important mindset you have probably already begun to incorporate into a shift is how you perceive the power of your own thoughts. This will continue to grow and get stronger, the more you honor the truth of your ability to create your own reality.

My intention for you is to always remember that your "present" is only a reflection of where you were *before* your shift to more conscious thinking – that is, before your new thoughts begin to manifest. This allows you to continue choosing new thoughts to create your new reality. Although the lag time is sometimes daunting, eventually your new thought-forms will become your new reality. So hang in there and don't give up.

If you continue to work with your own conscious and subconscious mind in this way, focusing on the positive will eventually become habit and you will forever, give up power struggles and shaming and blaming others, as you hone and fine-tune your own new patterns.

You've probably already noticed that as you have been able shift these critical mindsets, your relationship is getting better and better.

Ramping-Up Your Juiciness by Feeling the Difference Between Male & Female Energy

In my introduction to "HE♥RTGASM!," I said that a woman can come from her feminine juiciness, and a man can use his focused attention, to bring sex to whole new levels of ecstasy. Now understanding honoring your male and female "differences," I hope this book has led you to celebrate your polarities, and indeed to open up vast possibilities in your love life that didn't exist before. *Vive la Difference!*

Trusting Your Passion as You Learn Orgasmic Response and Build Your Ecstatic Energy

You are probably having fun exploring your newly found pleasure centers and trying all kinds of sophisticated, exciting, and orgasmic sexual play you never dared to try before now.

And more importantly, I hope you have seen that you can truly get to the place where relating in your every day lives together is a joy, and your sex life pleasure meter is rising off the scale.

If you have already begun to see your power struggles crumbling into dust as they are replaced by true love and respect, you are well on your way to a truly sacred relationship. You have become a "Soul Couple," making your way along your combined soul's journeys. Hurray!

Afterword

Please Keep in Touch with Me

My book "Darlings," — now that you've finished "He♥rtgasm!," I'll miss your energy and loving thoughts.

The best way to stay in touch is by going to www.relatelovesex.com/, taking you to a page where you can add your name and email to my email list. By doing this, you'll automatically be subscribed to my *"chock full of valuable content"* monthly newsletter, and receive three free gifts which you can download or access immediately including:

- An exclusive link to the "sexy part" of my "Tantric Partner Yoga" DVD

- My 'HE♥RTGASM' Action-Processes" (used in my workshops and assembled from this book)

- My article, "Tantra & the Light," — How moving spiritual energy combined with physical techniques can produce a connection to Divine ecstasy

Also, if you want to continue to benefit and build on what you've learned in "He♥rtgasm!," and feel inspired to contact me about my counseling sessions and packages, the best way is to join my list first – then take the quick survey. If we're a fit, we'll contact you about having qualified for a free 15-minute strategy call, to see where we can go from there.

Also, from time to time you'll be receiving emails from me just to keep you up do date on what I'm doing. I've planned lots of juicy things in which you can participate in the future.

My intent for you is that you grow in love and in your connection to the Divine in all your relationships.

Love and Blessings,
Toni

P.S. You might find it helpful in establishing more intimacy in your relationship to do some simple 'partner yoga' contact with your lover as presented in my DVD, "Tantric Partner Yoga," — found at: www.tantrapartneryoga.com

What's Coming Next

Many years ago I wrote a book called "*The California Way to Natural Beauty*," featuring a holistic approach to health. The synergy of mind-body-spirit is a mindset that has always been at the forefront of everything I write, and is the modality for how I live my own life.

Having a healthy lifestyle includes a healthy diet, exercise, possibly taking nutritional supplements, and of course, a healthy state of mind.

There are some things that are out of the scope of "HE♥RTGASM!" that might need to be addressed as considerations in having a healthy relationship: Sometimes people's problems stem from chemical or mental imbalances that can often be solved with natural or allopathic medicine and/or treatment.

Recently I heard an interview with Daniel G. Amen, MD, an award-winning physician, psychiatrist, best-selling author, international speaker, and brain enhancement expert. He talked about the importance of brain health and the impact of the brain on every aspect of life, including your relationships. If you think your relationship problems might be partly the result of chemical imbalances, brain science is something that you might check into to help improve your everyday life.

Another innovator in the field of brain science is John Assaraff, who has compiled an amazing array of material related to activating the parts of the brain that can help you to eradicate ingrained patterns you might have found difficult to deal with on your own. Additionally, his presentations include training on how to stimulate and magnify your brainpower. John lectures extensively around the world on The Neuroscience of Success and achieving Peak Personal Performance.

Because the mental/psychological advantage of feeling good about yourself is so important for self-esteem in all your relationships, I will soon be creating a series of DVDs and a book on revolutionary scientific advancements for rejuvenation and age reversal.

End of Book Quiz

There are no right or wrong answers to these questions. They were created simply to get you thinking about how you would handle the following situations having read "HE♥RTGASM!."

The most creative and insightful answers will be published in my newsletter and the award for the "Best Answers" will be free attendance to one of my Relate>Love>Sex workshops or teleseminar series.

Feel free to role-play when answering these questions if they don't apply to you directly:

1. You are on the verge of a possible divorce and your husband is resistant to the ideas in this book. What will you do?

2. The two critical mindsets for making your relationship work require a shift to a more spiritual point of view. You are spiritually inclined, but your boyfriend really doesn't believe in "all that stuff." Are you going to try to convince him to give it a try anyway?

3. After a couple of break-ups with an abusive partner you are a bit "gun shy" of getting into another relationship – maybe not for a few more years. But you meet a wonderful guy who appears to have all the right stuff. What are you going to do?

4. Your last spouse was happy to play the typical housewife role and now you've met a woman who will have none of that because she works full time

and thinks that because you work at home, that you should take on the "wife" role. How will you handle her request?

5. You think that things have been going well for the two of you for years, but one day, he/she comes home and informs you that he/she is leaving you for someone else. What are you going to do?

6. The single life seemed to be your fate until one day you fall in love with someone from another culture who doesn't share your spiritual ideas and lifestyle, but who loves you too. What will you do?

7. You would love to meet your soul-mate but every time you hit it off with someone, the love just seems to dissolve. How can you get past this pattern of always attracting "the wrong person"?

8. The love of your life has passed away and you just can't seem to shake off the grief and loneliness from your loss. You've met someone who is smitten with you, but you just aren't sure you are ready to get involved in another relationship. How do you plan to handle this situation?

9. Things are going well for both of you, but your love life isn't as exciting as it was in the beginning. This book has inspired you to try some new things with your beloved. Which ones will you try first?

Please email your answers to these questions to www.relatelovesex.com/quiz.contest

Appendix

EDWENE GAINES INTERVIEW
21 Day Challenge

Toni Interviews Edwene Gaines

Author and speaker, Edwene Gaines, is perhaps best known for her book, "The Four Spiritual Laws of Prosperity." She is also an ordained Unity minister since 1979, and is the owner and director of Rock Ridge Retreat Center in Valley Head, Alabama. She travels extensively, speaking and presenting prosperity workshops.

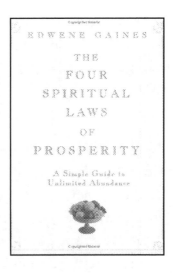

Through her books, workshops, and speaking engagements, she teaches and inspires people to know that God is our source, and that we live in a rich, abundant and generous Universe. It is with great humor and joy, that she shares the four spiritual principles of prosperity.

T. Hi Edwene. First of all, I was so impressed with your book. I want to tell you, I *love* your little book. I read it all the way through in one big "one-day lump." And then I highlighted all the places that I wanted to go back to. I worked with different things in the book for months and months and finally I just got to where I didn't have to do it anymore. One of the things that I had such a great time with was the 21-day challenge. As a matter of fact, in the book that I've just written — basically I was just so taken with the idea of the 21-day challenge that I put it in the book, and I hope I have your permission to do that — to use your name.

E. Of course.

T. This interview is going to be at the end of the book, in the Appendix section. There'll be an interview with you, and one with Will Bowen. I like what you are both doing — I think it's great. So let's get back to the 21-day challenge. How did you come up with that idea?

E. Well, I don't know specifically what happened, but it's along the line of — if you can do anything for a period of 21 days, then it becomes a part of the way you approach your world every day. And, somehow, when I complain, I am giving away my power, because what ever I'm saying, I don't like that whiny, complaining voice, which goes something like this, "Okay, I didn't do this, something did this to me — I am at the effect of something, I am not the cause, so it makes me feel powerless."

So what ever was happening might seem like a challenge. I learned to say instead, "I can hardly wait to see what good comes out of this."

T. I love that.

E. Yeah, it's a wonderful feeling to know that, "Maybe I *did* make this mess, but I also had the power to clean it up and I refused to give away my power ever again." Whatever's going on, if I don't like it then I fix it or I ask for assistance in fixing it, or I quit resisting it. And a wonderful thing begins to happen. It feels to me, that if we let go of using that energy to complain, what happens is we have a whole lot more energy to create and to express our gratitude, and move into making our world the way we want it to be.

What happens to me is when I find myself in one of those days where everything seems to go wrong — you stub your toe, your refrigerator breaks down, your dog messes up your new rug — whatever. Then you realize, huh, I could spend my whole life in negativity around this, or I can create my world the way I want it to be. And things began to shift. Now, I'm not saying that I never ever complain — every once in a while, one will just slip out, and I'll start out all over again, but now it gets noticed when I do this, and I'll notice how I'm sending my energy. It's a wonderful process for me and I want to share it with other people.

T. Well, that's a great answer to that question. And I *also* have felt that — when I catch myself whining I feel like a victim, and I don't want the world or me to think of myself as a victim. Because of you, and the things you said in this book, I catch things so much faster than before.

E. That is so true.

T. And I went through the same thing you went through when I stopped complaining and I didn't have anything to talk about.

E. I know, and that's a very dismal feeling, when you know that everything that's going on in your head — you can't really let it get out of your mouth, you know? I'm walking around in a daze, smiling at people, kind of a fake smile. Because I want to say something, and I have to tell you that once or twice I did this. And oh Toni, I'm not someone who complains, but if I *were,* no telling what I'd say. Oh, God, you know, we are all learning together and we're going to get there.

T. Yes, and I like that we're all learning together. That's why I think that the more people who spread this message, the better. I was just talking to a girl friend of mine, who said, "Wasn't it Dale Carnegie, who wrote the book, 'How to Win Friends and Influence People'? Didn't he say there were three "C's" — no complaining no criticizing and no condemning?"

E. Yes, yes — condemning, that's the word. Those are powerful, all of those — very powerful because, when we think about what those mean, if we make someone else responsible, other than ourselves (I don't mean to say that we are at fault or we are to blame), but we are, consciously or unconsciously, creating our world with every thought we think, every word we speak, and with every action we take, and so we have to be responsible with what we create.

So if you keep complaining and complaining, criticizing and criticizing, then you're going to find more to complain about because you'll find people are criticizing and condemning you. So you know very well, that whatever we send out, comes right back to us.

T. That's right — Hallelujah!

E. Send out the good stuff. I want the good stuff!

T. Me too, and if everybody's sending that out it's *got* to become a better world.

E. Someone once told me that nobody ever forgets a genuine compliment, and so instead of condemning, if we could just find some sweet, kind, honest thing to say to someone, it shifts the energy completely.

T. Yes I totally agree. It's a wonderful thing. So, Edwene I've seen you in some of those little videos on YouTube and, although I've never seen you in person, I was recently at a Lisa Sasevich seminar, and walked into the ballroom one Sunday morning, and there you were, on this huge screen. You are so funny! You are just so wonderful, and I want everybody to find out about you. I hope having this interview in my book is just one more way to add to the popularity that you already have.

E. I appreciate that so much Toni and my prayers are with you and all your wonderful projects.

T. Well, thank you. You travel something like 265 days a year, right?

E. About 250 days a year, and I'm going to start slowing down pretty soon. I just got in from Chicago yesterday, and I'm going to California on Friday — my itinerary is on my webpage. You probably already saw the dot com. And I do about 10 retreats here at my retreat center in North Alabama every year, usually three days — Friday Saturday Sunday. I teach you how to walk on fire and we j just have a wonderful time — we also have a wonderful set. We've been doing this for about 20 years and always have a great time.

T. Well! I didn't know you did all that. I actually walked on fire with Tony Robbins once years ago.

E. Wonderful. Tony and I studied with the same teacher, the founder of the fire walking movement, Tolly Burkan. I do mine little bit different than Tony does, as an initiation into what you might be familiar with — the work of Imogen Hopkins and her book, "High Mysticism," and she talked about the affirmations that you might use. One of them is, "I am one with the miracle-working presence." I use the fire walk as sort of an introduction to your ability to do miracles in your work. And if you can walk on fire, which most of the world thinks is impossible, there's nothing that can stop you.

T. Yes, right!

E. It's powerful isn't it?

T. Very powerful. And it *does* make you feel like you can create miracles. I do it every day.

E. Of course. Absolutely.

T. And we *all* do it, except sometimes we're asking for something we don't want, through complaining and all that stuff, and we wonder why things aren't going very well.

E. For sure, and what part of the world do you live in?

T. I live in — almost the center of Los Angeles, in a little town called Culver City.

E. Oh yeah, that's where Michael Beckwith is.

T. That's right, I actually live about five minutes from Michael's church, Agape.

E. He has a good venue about my workshop on his website, and I get fan mail from people from all over the world. It's so amazing!

T. I'll have to look into that.

E. Yeah, it's been very powerful. I just got a letter yesterday from Amsterdam and one from South Wales and one from France — they're tuning in — the world is waking up quickly.

T. Yay! Isn't that wonderful? Anyway I can tell people how to get a hold of you and tell them to watch your videos.

Well, I'm so happy you took the time to speak with us today, Edwene. For my part, I think everything you said was great and wonderful and I really appreciate that you've taken time out of your day to do this.

E. Well, you're so welcome and I know you're going to do well with this. It's a great work, and I feel very happy to be a part of it.

T. Thank you, and when are you going to be out here?

E. I go to California very frequently, and on my itinerary I have several California trips this year.

T. I would love to be at one of your events. One more thing, are you a Unity minister?

E. Yes, and I've been a Unity minister for 43 years.

T. Great, all right, I'll see you here in California when you get there.

E. Thank you, Toni, goodbye.

T. Bye for now...

REV WILL BOWEN INTERVIEW

Toni Interviews Reverend Will Bowen

Rev. Will Bowen is the creator and inspirational teacher of his own ministry called InVision. Additionally he is the author of the bestselling book, "A Complaint Free World." He is also a professional speaker whose main subject is about how to reverse habitual complaining (which prevents us from experiencing success) based on Edwene Gaines, "21 Day Challenge," and through using a device that he calls the "Complaint-free World" wristband. He says, "We believe that everyone deserves to live a happy, healthy, peaceful and prosperous life and we provide you with the resources to make this a reality."

T. Hi Will. I'm looking at two *really* handsome pictures of you — you're a very good-looking guy.

W. Well coming from you that's high praise.

T. Thanks, Will. In 2006 you started a campaign to have a complaint free world. What was the basis of this idea?

W. I was doing a series based on Edwene Gaines' book, "The Four Spiritual Laws of Prosperity," and Edwene was actually the person who recommended that people try and go 21 days without complaining. She says people say they want to be more prosperous in their lives but they complain about what they currently have. The twist that I was able to put on it was a way of monitoring people's success towards going 21 days, which was utilizing the 21-day complaint-free bracelet.

T. Well, tell us more about the bracelet.

W. The bracelet is made from a strong silicone — actually it's a purple bracelet — you put it on either wrist. Every time you catch yourself complaining you switch it to the other wrist. Of course the goal is to go 21 days, so this way you can monitor your progress. So when you put it on your wrist, you're on Day One, if you complain, or *when* you complain, you switch to the other wrist, and you are back on Day One. To date, we've sent out over 10 million bracelets to 106 countries.

T. That's amazing. I think it's a great idea, in fact I think it's such a great idea that I'm going to be doing something similar myself, and I'm giving both you and Edwene tons of credit for it — Your interviews are going to be in the appendix of my book, so that's really great. I think that the more people that are doing this, the better.

W. Absolutely.

T. When you're sending out these bracelets, do people pay for them? How does that work?

W. We generally offered them as free, and then we asked people to make donations, but unfortunately, when we were on the Oprah Winfrey Show we had over 2 million requests in 24 hours, and of course, we needed the money to actually *buy* the bracelets and ship them and we didn't have the money, so we switched to a pay model — $10 for 10 bracelets, and that includes shipping.

T. So what did you *do* with that — two million bracelets? — How did you rectify that?

W. Well honestly, we tried for many months to actually get — to get things and our financial situation resolved so we could send them out. And ultimately we just had to email everybody and tell them the truth. Most people make a donation, but only after they receive the bracelets. And since we didn't have the money to send the bracelets, we were going to have to switch to a pay model, and I would say that 98% of the people, said "No problem, here's the money," and they ordered the bracelets and we were able to turn it around and ship them out.

T. That's so great — I <u>love</u> that story!

When you actually did the challenge yourself, the first time you heard about it, how long did it take you to get through it?

W. It took me three and a half months to go through 21 consecutive days without complaining.

T. That's about how long it took me, actually. It seemed to take a very long time.

W. It takes most people about that long.

T. Oh what a great learning process. And do you find that either yourself or with other people that you talk to, that there's a falling off — after the initial phase of having done the 21 days?

W. Not so much — it pretty much becomes habitual, and that people end up staying with it once it's become a habit. If you go three to eight months watching everything that you say — everything that comes out of your mouth, it can become absolutely transformative. I'm sure there are some people who slip back, but then I also hear people who say that they're going to do the program again. The interesting thing is that if it took them three to eight months the first time to do the 21 consecutive days, then the second time takes very little time.

T. Right — that makes total sense. I *have* found that a couple of times over the last few months, that I've had a couple of things come out my mouth, like gossiping. I hate doing it but sometimes when I'm with a bunch of girlfriends, and someone's name comes up, and we start talking about them, and all of sudden I go, "Whoops — I wish I hadn't said that."

It is hard, at least for me, to always remember to do that. One of the other things I try to do is not even *think* negative thoughts, and of course every time I catch myself *thinking* negative thoughts, I just reframe it and put it back in a different way. And I think that works out pretty well too, because it's sort of cancels out anything you set in motion by even *thinking* negatively. Do you agree?

W. Absolutely, I *do* think though, that with us thinking somewhere around 70,000 thoughts a day (which is what the latest experts say), then it's probably much easier for you to catch and change the words we say, and what I find is (and what people have told me is) that by catching their words, they ultimately retrain their mind, by over and over again realizing that they can't speak unless there is something positive — their minds literally begin to shift.

T. Right. So did you find that you went through of period of time where you felt that you had nothing to talk about while you were still practicing?

W. Yes, I did — I don't think I did quite so much as some people. I know of a family who said they sat at the dinner table for about a week and they had nothing to talk about, because everything they started to say — they realized they were going to have to switch their bracelets, and so they chose not to.

T. Wow — great story! I love that. You must have gotten lots of stories from people over the years about their experience with the bracelets. Do you have a favorite story?

W. Probably my favorite one was from a prison guard in New York, a woman, and her job was to take care of or serve the people there — who would spit at her, cuss at her, throw things at her — attack her. Then she did the 21-day challenge and in the end, when she finally made it, her family threw her a party and they asked her what had changed, and she said, "You know the interesting thing is, I never told any of the prisoners that I was doing this. But the prisoners treat me better now because it's as if they can sense my positive energy and they don't respond in negative and hurtful ways."

T. Oh, that's great! Just for the benefit of the general public, please explain how complaining prevents us from experiencing success?

W. Well complaining keeps us focused on the problem rather than looking for solutions. That's the main thing — it perpetuates our negativity. And as Eckhart Tolle says, it stimulates our "pain body." Everybody has a pain body. We experience life through either joy or through pain. We only know we're alive through our sensations that we're feeling — like as I'm sitting here, I'm feeling the wind go by, I'm sensing sounds I'm hearing — so that's how we sense life. A lot of people experience life negatively. They only know how to do *that*. And complaining puts themselves on guard if things are not good. So unfortunately, by focusing on what is wrong, they attract *to* them what is wrong, and they perpetuate it.

T. I'm so glad to hear you say that, because my next question was going to be about how this relates to the law of attraction, which I think many of us practiced before the law of attraction became popular through the movie, The Secret. Is there anything else you want to say on that subject before my next question?

W. No, I mean it's just that you can't be talking about the way things "are," and complaining about them too, without perpetuating them because what is, is what was, and what is now, is what you were thinking about, focusing on, and talking about. Therefore if you change what you're thinking about or focusing on, and talking about now, you will change what comes in the future.

T. Yes, that's great.

So, maybe our readers would like to hear about how not complaining helps us to be more grateful and appreciative. Do you have anything to say about that?

W. Well, the opposite of complaining is gratitude, and in fact, twice now we have had members of Congress introduce bills to declare the day before Thanksgiving, Wednesday the 23rd, to be a complaint free day in the United States.

It was interesting, because they could get no other members of Congress, to sign on and support it, because Congress, in many ways, *lives* off negativity and complaining. They have to make problems so that *they* can be the solution *to* the problems, and it's a way of building power. People complain for five reasons, and one of the main reasons people complain is to gain power. The opposite of complaining is gratitude and the more we shift from talking about what we don't want, to talking about what we *do* want, the more we experience that in our lives.

T. Yes, I think that's absolutely true. Well, what are the other four reasons, besides to get more power?

W. Well, people complain for five reasons: they complain to get attention, they complain to remove themselves from responsibility, they complain to brag or inspire envy, they complain for power, and they complain to excuse their poor performance. Those are the five reasons that scientists have found and everything I have seen supports that. I've never been able to find anything that falls outside of one of those five categories.

T. Fantastic! I imagine that you've published a great deal of this in your newest book — is that also called "A Complaint Free World"? Or does it have a different title?

W. Well, actually I have two new books coming out this year but one of them is an updated version of "A Complaint Free World," but yes.

T. And what was the other one?

W. The other one is called "Happy This Year — the Secret of Getting Happy Once and for All."

T. Great. So when can people find that?

W. It will be available between Christmas and the New Year, published by Amazon — they have a new spiritual imprint coming out and they don't actually have a name for it, but the publisher is Amazon.

T. We'll let people know about that. Are you still a minister of the Unity Church?

W. No, I've started my own ministry called InVision.

T. That's wonderful. Do you have a following in InVision right now or are you just beginning it?

W. No, we have services every week.

T. And did you sort of transfer what you were doing before to the same group of people or are you attracting a whole new crowd now?

W. Both actually, we've had a number of people who left the old church, and are with me, including our band, and we have continued, and have had a number of new people who came along.

T. You have a band too?

W. Yes, the band from the church that provides music.

T. That sounds exciting — a little bit like Agape, huh?

W. Very much like Agape, yes.

T. Wonderful. Well one of these days...

Where are you now, so I can come out and see you one day, and experience your church?

W. Kansas City, Missouri.

T. Okay, wonderful. And is that the main thing you are doing there? Do you have anything new you've added to your menu?

W. Well, I do that plus I write, pretty much full time, and I also travel and do a lot of corporate speaking engagements.

T. Do you want people to know how to reach you?

W. Sure, they can reach me at Will@complaintfreeworld.org.

T. Okay, I guess that's all for right now, Will, unless you have anything else to add or unless you have any questions to ask me.

W. No, I've looked at your website, and I think I know pretty much about everything that's going on, so, no. This is great — I appreciate the opportunity.

T. Alright, I hope we'll talk again another time. Thank you so much, Will.

W. Thank you too, Toni, bye-bye.

More Information About the "Heartgasm! 21 Day Challenge" Bracelets/Wristbands

We plan to be working with a non-profit organization that will be the recipient of our tithing funds – i.e. any profit we see from the sales of the bracelet after our costs have been recouped.

You can send an email to www.relatelovesex.com/ wristbands requesting a price sheet and the models of the bracelets/wristbands that are available.

The photos below are the primary ones we will be distributing with possible variations on the colors.

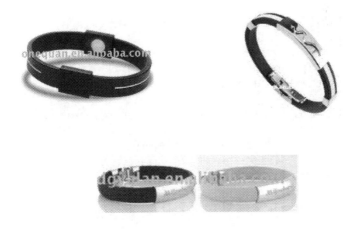

Elizabeth Barrett Browning's Poem

Love – How Can I Count the Ways?

In this famous quote, "How do I love thee? Let me count the ways," from an Elizabeth Barrett Browning poem – instead of thinking of this as an ode to another person, you might think of it as a 'love proclamation' to yourself – or at least your higher self:

How do I love thee? Let me count the ways.

I love thee to the depth and breadth and height

My soul can reach, when feeling out of sight

For the ends of Being and ideal Grace.

I love thee to the level of everyday's

Most quiet need, by sun and candle-light.

I love thee freely, as men strive for Right;

I love thee purely, as they turn from Praise.

I love thee with a passion put to use

In my old griefs, and with my childhood's faith.

I love thee with a love I seemed to lose

With my lost saints, –- I love thee with the breath,

Smiles, tears, of all my life! – and, if God choose,

I shall but love thee better after death.